like,
comment,
share,
buy

like, comment, share, buy

the beginner's guide to marketing your business with video storytelling

jonathan creek

WILEY

First published in 2021 by John Wiley & Sons Australia, Ltd

42 McDougall St, Milton Qld 4064
Office also in Melbourne

Typeset in Garamond Premier Pro 11.5pt/14pt

ISBN: 978-0-730-39001-5

A catalogue record for this book is available from the National Library of Australia

Cover design by Wiley

Cover Image: © Tamara Midonova/Shutterstock; © Giamportone/Shutterstock

Internal control graphics: © lilipom / Getty Images

Printed in Singapore by Markono Print Media Pte Ltd

SKY7A32E09F-EE82-48B8-A56E-28750B50A0AE_122220

Disclaimer
The material in this publication is of the nature of general comment only, and does not represent professional advice. It is not intended to provide specific guidance for particular circumstances and it should not be relied on as the basis for any decision to take action or not take action on any matter which it covers. Readers should obtain professional advice where appropriate, before making any such decision. To the maximum extent permitted by law, the author and publisher disclaim all responsibility and liability to any person, arising directly or indirectly from any person taking or not taking action based on the information in this publication.

To my beautiful wife and my daughters, PK and EZ,
for your unwavering support while I chase my curiosities.

This work is as much yours as it is mine.

contents

foreword

Perhaps you've grabbed this book because you want to find better ways to capture moments and create milestones, both personal and professional. Or you want to learn how to create better video content to advance your career or draw you nearer to family and friends. The great news is, whether you want to create videos that win more heart share at your place or greater market share in the professional space, you have an invaluable resource here that will help you be more 'resourceful' in this endeavour.

It's clear that video today is the go-to medium for capturing moments and projecting messages in every sense. Indeed, nothing offers a professional or their business greater 'cut-through' than video. Ever since smart phones gave everyone the capacity to be a videographer and YouTube provided the perfect platform to be a broadcaster, video content has grown exponentially across the globe. And professionals and influencers have increasingly looked for ways to generate 'brand awareness' with enhanced video content.

Consider these compelling numbers for a moment. More than 500 hours of video is uploaded on YouTube *every minute*. That's more than all of the video content on Facebook and Netflix combined being consumed every day. To stand out in this overpopulated space presents a daunting challenge. Yet the knowledge that more than 1 billion hours of YouTube videos are consumed every 24 hours across the globe compels us to enter and attempt to make an impact in this crowded space.

You are about to learn a powerful formula that, once applied and followed, can help you create an emotional connection with your audience and spread your message, product or brand 'at the speed of a click'. The principles are extremely easy to learn and even easier to implement. That's because they are introduced by an absolute expert in the field. Someone who has dedicated a fair chunk of his professional life to discovering the 'code' that makes certain videos go viral and has simplified its application, enabling you to reach well beyond your local network. I'm certain that once you understand the 'Spread Factor' that underpins all of Jonathan's work, you will never look at video content the same way again!

Jonathan Creek is a true educator who possesses the rare ability to take a complex message and make it simple enough for anyone to understand. I have seen him hold the emotional connection with audiences at major conferences, as well as smaller groups, as he shares the nuances of his time-tested formula. He will coach you through the same principles as you work through this book. These principles have helped thousands of people reposition their business, widen their audience reach and monetise their networks. I have personally benefited from Jonathan's teachings in all of these areas, and gained a friend in the process.

The real gift of Jonathan's work, as I see it, is that while his fundamentals work when fully applied, you don't have to change who you are, or pretend to be something you're not, to ensure your videos soar into the social media stratosphere. At the heart of Jonathan's message is the key ingredient of authenticity. The world needs more authentic people crafting value-added content that forms a positive emotional connection.

Many people search YouTube to find out how to do things they have never done before. In 'Creeky', you have found a coach who will enhance your video methodology one lesson at a time to a level you've never reached before. I hope you find this process as powerful, beneficial and rewarding as I have in the past, and as I continue to do every day.

Rik Rushton, author of *The Power of Connection*

Without a plan your videos are simply a mash of pretty pixels and white noise.

author's note

I know this is a big call but ... the internet needs saving, and I need your help to do it.

But before I ask you to surrender your old ways, to start thinking differently and lean into the possibilities that exist on social media, let me frame the real problem.

Video executed well can change your life; after all, as I'll lay out in this book, it can be the most powerful content on the internet. Video done poorly, though, can bury your business.

The problem is that while everyone has access to video-making tools these days, most don't know how to take advantage of it. There are too many Karens and Darrens sweating the small stuff, too many politicians pushing agendas, too many big-brand sales guys and girls ... just being pushy. The internet is drowning in boring, vanilla, corporate videos that fail to inspire, connect or convert anyone.

These types of videos are clogging newsfeeds, and this doesn't make for a great user experience. Big brands, big business shouldn't be able to 'win' the internet (or ruin it) simply because they have bigger advertising budgets. And people who make hundreds of videos a day shouldn't be able to dominate the space based on volume alone. To save the internet, it needs to stop — *they need to be stopped*. This is where you come in, and where this book comes in. Sure, making videos is important work, but you need to go about it the right way.

I don't know about you, but I love a good underdog story. When I was writing this book and thinking about my readers, it was the underdogs I had in mind. In every chapter I found myself coming back to the same challenging question: 'How can I help an entrepreneur or small business owner, armed only with the smartphone in his or her pocket, take on the big players with multimillion-dollar budgets in their space?'

Disruptive to its core. In fact, my goal was to create a disruptor's handbook to modern video marketing that is accessible to all, because I know for sure you don't need high-level video production skills to achieve success. The process I've developed and share with you here is easy to understand and simple to follow, but still gives you the tools you need to generate powerful change and achieve incredible results on next to no budget, or at least at a fraction of the cost of hiring an advertising agency.

The key lies in understanding what drives social media and the levers that exist to maintain it as a consumer-driven playground, along with a deep understanding of a potent form of content called viral video. This book, based on a decade of research and experience, explores the opportunities that are created when you combine the two understandings and how you can apply what you learn to your business regardless of your experience with a video camera. Before you've finished you'll be saying goodbye to those conventional, boring, even annoying promotional videos and creating your own contagious content that is guaranteed to inspire people to take action.

Along the way I'll also share with you:

- ► user behaviour strategies developed from my analysis of more than 1200 viral videos
- ► the secret ingredients to not only connecting with an audience but persuading them to share your message

- ▶ a lesson on storytelling I soaked up from Academy Award–winning Hollywood director James Cameron

- ▶ exercises for you to complete in order to start building your unique video foundations

- ▶ scannable QR codes to unlock viral videos referred to in the book. Watch them in real time as we discuss the key points and pivotal differences that made them a success.

Now, if you are feeling stuck on social media, your connections uncertain, your numbers not where you want to see them, before you throw in the towel, or throw away any more money on marketing, let me introduce you to the *Like, Comment, Share, Buy* approach. I'm certain it will change your thinking and even inspire you. Then you and I can start saving the internet, one bad video at a time.

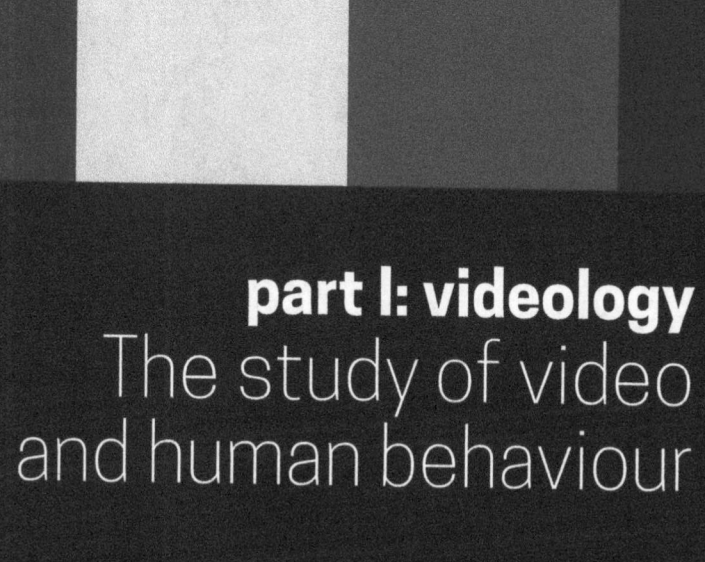

part I: videology
The study of video
and human behaviour

In the five chapters of Part I, the aim is to establish a common understanding, a place where you can still be uniquely you but our beliefs around the lay of the land are aligned. I'll share insights, observations and learnings that I have gleaned from my years of dissecting, testing and analysing video that spreads, and the powerful roles played by social platforms and humans in these interactions.

It all begins with the most valuable resource we can draw on, *human attention*, and how to capture and use it to your full advantage in both business and life, before introducing the new powerhouse in the attention space, the *viral video*.

The statement 'Content is King' is everywhere, but what does it mean, and is it true? Or is it just noise? We'll explore beyond the simple statement that gurus use to skip over what's needed, because it's a bit more complex than just doing. You can't just turn on a camera and expect your videos to magically work. Great videos need many aligned ingredients to be successful, and that's where viral videos come into it. We examine why and how they work.

Sharing is the most important ingredient of success in the new media world — it validates your content, and in turn your brand, service or product. Learn to understand the modern-day mystery of spreading your message and the key principles to getting it right.

At the top of the principles pile is one that, more than any other, is vital for success. Context. Without proper context embedded into your content you risk simply adding to the noise that already exists. So what is context? How do you identify it? And most importantly how do you communicate it to those who find it relevant? The answer starts with your purpose: identifying, extracting and focusing on the desires of your audience and then fulfilling them in a way that delivers real business outcomes, which is what this book is all about.

The *Like, Comment, Share, Buy* approach is based on a working formula that encourages you to think differently. This book introduces viable strategies that will be unique to you and easily implemented. In Hollywood it's 'Lights, Camera, Action'; in social media it's 'Likes, Comments, Action'. This is the sequence we will focus on so you can lead your way to the top using video marketing.

Now before you dive in, understand this one key difference. This book — the approach, the system, the Virable formula — is not one-size-fits-all. It's about your own particular journey. The work you do as you progress through the chapters will be unique to you, and that's a powerful thing. Your values, your insights, your experience and your story. It is important that you find the true you and your own business values.

Don't ever be afraid to be different.

chapter 1
the struggle for attention

How would capturing 1 million views on social media change your life? Would it make you rich? Famous? Would having a million views give you greater influence, in your business or personally?

The reality in today's world is that attracting enough views at the right time definitely gives you clout. Just as with popular movies, TV shows or public speaking, the more you can attract people's attention, the more people will stand still long enough to listen to what you have to say. If they like it, they'll be more likely to come back and listen to what you have to say next time. If they don't, they may *still* come back to check you out next time. However they feel, they will begin to rely on the value you deliver to help enrich their own knowledge and therefore their own public profile.

The game, the fame game, has been around since the amphitheatres of ancient Greece and Rome. What's new is the multitude of ways in which our messages can now be delivered, how we can reach crowds of almost unimaginable size, and the skills we need to master the arts of this mass communication. Get them right and you can influence a lot more people more easily than has ever been possible before. There has never been a better time to spread your message and increase the influence of your business and, ultimately, your bottom line.

It wasn't long ago that prime-time TV was the go-to platform for delivering a commercial message to the masses. But with the maturation of social media, the exponential growth of the digital audience and the evolution of the first generation of digital natives (whose entire lives have been dominated by digital communication), there is a new powerhouse in the attention space.

The new player, which sits at the pinnacle of attention-grabbing excellence, is the viral video.

For those who don't know, viral videos are online videos that seem to spread through a life force of their own. Once posted, for very specific reasons that I will explain in the course of this book, they trigger viewers to push them out to greater audiences by sharing, commenting and engaging with them. Audience interaction is the vital difference between videos that attract millions of views and others that attract none.

Anything video — my early experience

Understanding how to trigger this 'sharing' was the challenge that captured my attention with the growth of online video culture. During the early 2000s I was a TV journalist for Australia's biggest and most popular TV network. I was producing three or four stories a week for a public affairs show whose primary, unashamed focus was on attracting as much viewer attention as possible. Critics would often say this came at the expense of 'good' journalism. The truth is that unlike news reporting, where the structure of a story is

90 per cent predetermined, public affairs allowed for greater creativity, higher production values, more storytelling and, yes, often a bit of 'shock and awe' too.

I had at my disposal professional camera operators, editors, researchers, producers...and millions of dollars' worth of the latest technical equipment. I also had something of a captive audience. With only 10 TV channels, the Australian audience didn't have that much choice in what to watch. As a result, our show attracted a significant national audience of around 1.8 million viewers a night.

At the time, this put the show at the top of the ratings: it was a bulletproof, ever-reliable attention-grabbing machine. So much so that executives were totally unprepared for the approaching tsunami of Facebook, YouTube and the rest. Whenever these platforms, today's social media giants, were raised in conversation, the bosses dismissed them. They never anticipated a world in which anyone had the potential capacity to broadcast their own message to a global audience. They continued to ignore the advances in phone technology that led to HD cameras becoming standard issue. They didn't believe that mobile networks would be able to handle the data amounts it takes to deliver video affordably for the mass market. And they absolutely refused to believe the general public would be able to produce better content than they could. The truth they missed is that the world had changed. TV networks are no longer protected by expensive infrastructure and the high cost of entry. Their traditional advantages have evaporated; their business model is broken. YOU now wield the power. You can broadcast your own message and if you're good enough, you will attract *a million views*.

From the very beginning I found the internet intriguing. I had a cousin who was building chatrooms and online noticeboards that operated over the family phone lines in the late 1980s. I remember my mum and aunty never being able to speak because the computers had taken the phones offline. By the time my cousin was in his late teens, those hobbies had grown into a significant business. This early exposure opened my eyes to the possibilities of the internet. But the thing was, I found no joy in chatrooms or coding. My real love was for anything video, especially storytelling and communicating, games and cameras. I loved video games that followed stories and I leapt at any chance to get closer to a video camera. Those chances were rare in the eighties. We certainly never owned one, so my exposure to the art of filming was restricted to sometimes at school getting to share a 15-minute window with four other kids, all of us recording on the same VHS tape. It was far from ideal, but it was enough to give me the video storytelling bug.

In my final year of school I learned I was the first student in the State of Victoria, if not Australia, to submit a final-year assignment on VHS tape. It was all shot and edited in camera. (And if anyone from the Victorian Education Department is reading this, I would love that tape back sometime.) My first job was in TV, as were my second and third, each step getting me closer to creating and producing stories using video. By the late nineties my two overriding interests — video and the internet — started to converge. I didn't know it at the time but this changed things; it changed humans, the way we communicate and interact and, most important to my mind, the way we *share*.

At first, online videos spread as tiny, low-res files attached to long email chains. Numbers of views weren't recorded. Their success was measured by how long the daisy chain of email addresses was, and also by word of mouth. Then came websites and forums with catalogues of links to videos. Those early sites led naturally to the creation of video platforms, the unrivalled king of which is YouTube.

Understandably, YouTube began as an unsophisticated, somewhat random platform without so much as a Share button — it was a matter of copying the URL and emailing the link around — but before too long, driven by its popularity, YouTube scaled, and it scaled hard. In 2005, Nike produced the first video to reach a million views. That milestone finally had media bosses and brands starting to take notice, albeit still half-heartedly, and even today not nearly enough.

As more and more videos reached that magic million-view milestone, it became the benchmark for 'success'. Not long after, the term 'viral video' was coined. I started to take note of the effects viral videos were having on the behaviours of those around me. Those water-cooler conversations about what they saw on TV last night had been replaced by huddles around a computer monitor to watch the latest trending video.

It was the beginning of the shift from 'word of mouth' and face-to-face exchanges to digital transactions. Two key moments fuelled the change in behaviours: the emergence of social media platforms and the simplification of 'sharing'. We no longer had to copy and paste, and risk sending something unrelated to work on our work email. There was another, safer, simpler way — and it didn't take long to catch on.

What fascinated me next in this period of transition was the emphasis experts placed on production quality. TV networks around the world thought they were safe from the onslaught of 'amateur' online video because high production values would save them. It's a belief many still cling to: audiences won't watch cheaply produced videos characterised by poorly framed, grainy images.

I too initially bought into the 'production values' myth. Never in my wildest dreams did I imagine a video made on a phone could attract millions more views than a piece produced by a team of experts armed with a practically bottomless budget. At the time it seemed axiomatic, and was certainly backed by the behaviour of advertising agencies and even Hollywood, that the bigger the budget the bigger the bang. I was wrong. Your budget will never guarantee you views. Don't believe me? Walk into your local camera store and tell them you want to buy the camera that's going to get you the most views on YouTube. In fact, just for the fun of it, record yourself doing this and share the video with me online.

The reality that a generous budget doesn't guarantee success hit me hard after I spent more than six months of risking my own personal safety for a story I believed was going to capture the attention of the Australian public. Six months of shady meetings using hidden cameras in junk yards, industrial area carparks and the backrooms of dingy cafés, endless email chains in several languages using fake profiles — all of which eventually led us to the Vietnam–Chinese border. I was chasing smugglers and the authorities were chasing us. The gangs that were illegally taking toxic products out of Australia and auctioning them on the wharves in Asia were the least of my worries. Ultimately the investigation cost tens of thousands of dollars of the company's money — for one six-minute story told using video. To say there was a lot riding on the ratings would be an understatement.

I remember walking into work the morning after that story went to air. I expected my colleagues' conversation to be dominated by this revelatory piece of investigative journalism. I imagined I'd be bombarded with questions about the parts we couldn't broadcast, the risks we took, the sinister truth we had revealed.

It never happened. My moment in the spotlight had been hijacked. Instead of my production being the centre of attention I arrived to find a crowd of my co-workers leaning over a computer watching a video on YouTube. It was grainy, noisy and badly produced — it wasn't even edited — yet it had their rapt attention. I found this behaviour baffling, even (I'm not going to lie) annoying, but also intriguing. Particularly as I watched as others began to arrive in the office. It was like everyone in the room vied to be the first to share this incredible video they had just watched. It was a kind of contest for kudos.

That realisation marked the start of this journey in search of an answer to a simple question:

Why do people share?

At the time I started this search, viral videos were already influential, but they weren't the alpha predators of the internet they are today. Still, I could see that they held great power because they were able to attract incredible levels of attention.

It was this influence that had me scrambling to work out how they did it. What are the mechanisms in the human brain that make us click Share?

Answering this question became the prime objective of my self-created PhD. It kept me awake many a night for years. And sharing some of the answers I discovered — answers that will help you dramatically increase the influence and effectiveness of your video content, no matter what your business — starts here.

You see, viral videos are a great way to learn because they are the best of breed. They also rely for success on human responses, and that's a power that social platforms have yet to control. So, regardless of what they do with the algorithms, if social media platforms want to stay in business, they have to keep accommodating the types of videos that not only capture our attention and encourage us to share their stories, but also trigger us to *act*.

So what makes people Like, Comment, Share and Buy?

Pay attention because attention pays

Human attention is the most valuable resource we can draw on.

We now live in an era in which individuals, brands and businesses live and die by the amount of attention they can secure — day in, day out.

Whether you are an entrepreneur launching your first start-up, a successful business owner, a consultant, or a social media or marketing manager taking care of the online persona of your business or brand, you won't survive if you keep producing content that doesn't take hold and drive real business results. The struggle for attention — to be seen and heard to the max — is at the very core of business in the 21st century.

The key is to ensure you don't waste a moment on creating content that doesn't help or support your cause. You need to start building your influence now to make sure you can keep up when the big brands start embracing, and spending, online. Mark Zuckerberg wants Facebook to be 85 per cent video content by the end of 2021. A Facebook executive in Europe went a step further: citing the speed with which video has become a 'megatrend', she sees the platform on the path to becoming totally video content by 2022. Digital analytics data blog Tubular has predicted that the internet will be 80 per cent video by 2021.

There is no doubt that the video era is now. And at the pace things are moving it is surely the gateway to what's coming next — virtual and augmented reality. But here's a fundamental truth: VR and AR are complex variations of reality. While video is by far the most influential online content, it's still relatively easy to make crap videos. If you don't first master storytelling using conventional video, it's going to be even harder for you to create effective stories via alternate realities.

Take a moment to let that sink in, because I believe it's really important. If you don't take the necessary steps to master video communication now, you have little chance of successfully exploiting the new technologies that are already on their way. And what that means for business is that within five short years you may not have enough of the world's attention to be running a viable business.

So what does it take to master communicating with video? I asked myself this question when I first started searching for the holy grail solution to creating viral videos. Attention is the answer most people throw out there, but I can share with you that it is only part of the answer. TV still demands attention from generally passive viewers, but right now TV is facing its greatest challenge since taking on the radio industry. Viral videos are way more efficient at holding our attention than any other form of media. They can rack up millions of views with little to no budget and accurately target any demographic, guaranteeing high relevance scores. The way they spread isn't through attention alone; the successful spread depends on actions. Platforms reward engagement and interactions, and if you want to go viral your content needs to trigger those responses.

The question is how? I wrote this book to help you answer this question and negotiate this struggle, and to share with you what I have learned from two decades of making videos almost every day and five years spent researching viral videos.

Viral videos are truly the most powerful force on the internet, racking up millions of views, and thousands of comments and shares. If you're going to spend time learning something new, you may as well learn from the best. Viral videos are the best. They set the gold standard when it comes to engaging and influencing large audiences. This book takes us on a journey to revealing their secrets.

In the chapters that follow I'll walk you through the steps you need to take to create viral content, recognising that this will be a process that is unique to every individual, brand or business. For it to succeed, it has to be.

But before we begin our deep dive, I'll introduce a few basic concepts we'll be exploring that you may not be completely familiar with. I also want to offer a little context in relation to my research conclusions — what sets them apart and my process in drawing them up. This book offers practical insights into how you can apply the knowledge I gained from my own research, testing and observations, which included speaking with leading psychologists, human behaviourists, marketers... and even Hollywood producers.

Out of my research I developed the Virable™ formula, an algorithm that measures whether or not, and how far, a video will spread.

I speak often about Virable on stages around the world and now rely on it to help businesses thrive. You might say we use it in much the same way that supermarket chains conduct taste testing. Rather than measuring whether they like or would buy something as a result of seeing it, we test the instinctive human response around sharing. It calculates what I call the *Spread Factor*™, a measure that can be applied to all viral videos.

I identified the Spread Factor after analysing more than 1200 of the world's most-viewed videos. The Virable formula is an approach I've been teaching to leading brands, companies and even individuals ever since. It has helped people gain more followers and sell more products. Most importantly, it has helped them not only to hold a greater share of people's attention but also to hold it for longer than ever before.

Just being familiar with the Spread Factor idea offers businesses a massive advantage. Even more powerful is that once you understand the complete Virable formula you can reverse engineer it to determine any areas in which your videos fall short — that is, where they are failing to hold the audience's attention. Once you apply the formula to the stories you tell, you will no longer waste precious time and money creating videos that your audiences ignore.

Great videos are hard to make, no doubt about it. And it's soul destroying when all that hard work generates little by way of results. The Virable approach offers a step-by-step guide to how to avoid any more of those costly failures. As a result, your storytelling content creation will become more efficient and more potent.

Why do viral videos work? — a brief insight

To understand viral videos better you first need to grasp how they work. What is it that they possess that 99.99 per cent of other videos don't?

There are three unique things all viral videos do:

1. **They capture the attention of a large, broad-based audience.** They seize and align with a critical event or moment in time and ride it like a wave, but rather than burning out after a while they create their own momentum, becoming a force unto themselves.

2. **They hold that attention.** Duration isn't a factor, so while the gurus are telling you to keep your videos short, viral videos are suggesting the opposite by actually holding viewers' attention for longer.

   Relying on 'average view times' as a guide is a bad idea. A platform may host a million bad videos that their audience stops watching after an average of five seconds. Obviously this doesn't mean your videos should be no more than five seconds long, but rather that you need to capture your audience's attention within five seconds or they may stop watching. An entirely different lesson.

3. **They involve an exchange.** Rather than being a passive experience they are interactive, and understanding this is vital to your success. Viral videos create an environment that triggers an audience instinctively to act. It is this response or action that starts the viral cycle. So you should always start making your videos with this end in sight. What is it you want your viewers to do? Where are you taking them and how do you want them to react? Simply giving them information is never going to be enough.

Remember, there is more video content in the world than ever before, so simply showing up with more and hoping for something to happen isn't enough. Audiences are more sophisticated — you need to be too.

Three differences that make all the difference

Before we start peeling back the layers, I want to address another common myth about viral videos.

It is a long-held belief that these videos are a product of 'dumb luck'. This is certainly true of some but not all, or even most of them. We've all seen those chance video captures when a camera just happens to be recording as something astonishing, freaky or incredibly funny happens. Videos like 'Charlie bit my finger' or the one where the expert was being interviewed live on the BBC and his kid, chased by the nanny, ran into the office while he was speaking earnestly on air.

These kinds of videos will continue to grow in number as more and more of us carry our phone cameras with us wherever we go. But here's the thing. The viral videos I'm focused on are something very different. These aren't videos that capture the unexpected or freak moment for the online world. The viral videos that grab my attention, the ones I dissected to unravel their secret code, the ones you can build yourself and benefit from, have been purposely engineered to be shared.

If they have been built to be shared and it works, then there must be a formula for their success. And if there's a formula for their success, then we can learn what it is and use it for our own success.

For most people on the planet, viral videos are still a mystery. I find it staggering, for instance, how many small business owners who are struggling to make a profit ask me to explain what they are, revealing how disconnected they are from the opportunities they can take advantage of in the world right now by exploring and innovating in the way they market their products and services. Instead, most of them are just doing the same old thing that got them into trouble to begin with but somehow expecting different outcomes. In fact, it goes even deeper: it tells me they haven't even bothered to research or pay attention to how the world's attention has shifted. And the urgency of the problem is delivered in the answer I always respond with: 'What's a viral video? It's the one thing that could save your business and secure your future.'

There is a real divide among brands that engineer 'viral brand videos'. Most try but fail, while those that succeed tend to do so repeatedly. So what is it that the repeat offenders know or have that others don't? Of course, the answer is plenty, but I know one thing it isn't, and that's luck.

What I can tell you is that top-ranking viral videos that capture the world's attention are difficult to create. It's why people like Mark Zuckerberg value them so very, very much. But here's the kicker for you: you don't need every video you make to be a runaway success for it to influence your business or positively affect your bottom line. Every video with an increased Spread Factor can deliver a greater return in reach, engagement and business. It all comes down to understanding your own Viral DNA.

Your Viral DNA is a code, unique to you or your brand, that attracts and connects with your audience. It's the reason they follow you online.

Each year YouTube releases their list of the top 10 most-watched videos — this is the viral video equivalent of the billboard charts. When YouTube was only four or five years old this most-watched chart was dominated by 'lucky' videos of freak accidents and random events. Fast forward to today and smart entrepreneurs and big brands are making their move. Interestingly, more often than not they aren't traditional big brands but savvy emerging brands that understand the new landscape and the power of attracting and cultivating your own audience. Think video games like Fortnite and Red Bull energy drinks, or even the Ultimate Fighting Championship (UFC). All are fighting hard to attract viral attention, and the fact that we all know who they are, even though they're still young pups, shows it's a strategy that's working. The question is, what are you doing in your business to take advantage of this same opportunity?

The trend being pioneered by these emerging brands proved to me that a model for viral success exists even in the absence of a one-script-fits-all formula. I just had to work out what it was.

The answer was far from obvious, which is why it took me more than five years to unlock it. Hours upon hours of late nights, early mornings and countless pep talks from the bathroom mirror later and the research is in. Two years of testing and applying what I had learned has resulted in millions of views for those who have followed the Virable approach.

Even just saying that gives me chills, because I know that for some of you what you learn in this book and how you apply it will change the course of your life. Hell yeah — it changed the course of mine!

Through the filter of a phone screen or desktop computer, videos that go viral show up in all shapes and sizes, varying vastly — different topics, different target audiences, different genres, different moods. Across the board. The full spectrum.

Some make you happy, others sad or angry, sometimes even bored. Some are sophisticated, big-budget, Hollywood-type productions, while others are shot on a phone. Some star gorgeous models and celebrities, while others feature everyday people. But every one of them contains a special sauce.

And that's where viral videos stand alone. They seriously affect and influence the human brain. It's not luck ... it's science.

The science involved in the Virable approach is often complex, as each video is influenced by many independent variables. To simplify things, without missing any of the key learnings, I have broken it down into three top-line processes:

1. attracting attention

2. holding attention

3. triggering action.

Each of these processes can be further broken down to reveal five milestones or levels of stimulation required to send a video viral. Fail to achieve the standard required on any of these five levels and your video will likely crash and burn.

While these three key processes look simple enough, they dive deep into the following sciences:

- the psychology that triggers people to share
- the inputs that influence human engagement
- the DNA pathways of viral content.

Two key terms I have touched on and will be referring to often are:

- **Spread Factor.** This is the unit by which the potency of a video is measured. The Virable algorithmic formula relies on the Spread Factor to rate whether or not people will share a video. This book is that formula reverse engineered so you can create videos (in fact, any type of content) that will not only cut through the noise but make your message more easily understood and trigger people to share it. And when those events occur in succession your video is certain to spread.

- **Viral DNA.** To achieve viral success, every brand, business or entrepreneur needs to apply a unique combination of the five measured elements of the Virable formula. We refer to this unique code as their Viral DNA.

Now you have been briefed on the art and science that drives viral videos, are you ready to dive deep? The keys to a new world await you.

recap:
THE ART AND SCIENCE OF
GRABBING PEOPLE'S ATTENTION

- Attention is a win–win for you and the platform your content is posted to.

- Attracting attention is both instinctive and science based. The only thing that has changed since the birth of humankind are the tools we use to capture it.

- Viral brand videos are not the product of dumb luck; their potential for success can be measured.

strategy

Long-term success on social media can only be achieved using evergreen approaches that benefit both the creator and the host.

Too often creators fall into the trap of focusing solely on their audience and treating the social platform hosting them as a second-class citizen. Make sure you consider the needs and wants of the platform.

Attention is the main stock all platforms are invested in, but how they measure it varies. Ensure you understand the differences, no matter how subtle.

chapter 2
content is king?

The internet has changed many things, but easily the biggest changes have been in how we communicate and how we consume what is communicated to us.

Social media is no longer the new kid on the block. Facebook, Instagram, YouTube, Twitter, Twitch, TikTok and many more platforms that come and go are part of the new normal, and as they've matured they've changed the way we live and interact. Call it evolution, call it an addiction, but you can't call it a fad. Social media is here to stay and the advantage it has over all other media forms that preceded it is in the way it rapidly and constantly evolves. Combine social media's ability to change with the fact that almost anyone on the planet can access it, and you have a domain worth investing your time in.

For too long the focus has been on social media forms when it should have been on *content*. You simply can't be successful with social media without focusing on content.

The fact that you are reading this book tells me you already understand that the time to focus on being your own broadcaster starts now. So what does it mean to be a broadcaster? It means more than uploading a few posts here and there. It means being committed to an audience, always showing up and constantly delivering value.

Success in the new media world doesn't come from using scheduling bots to religiously post three, six or 50 times a day. Success isn't decided by hashtags. And it doesn't come from copying the latest trends — in fact, make that the first note you write down here. Copying the creative videos that have already gone viral will only cause you damage. Success or failure in this game comes down to the experience you provide, the level of activity you can stimulate in someone's brain. The question you should always be asking yourself is are you providing enough stimulation in the content you are delivering? Are you making people care?

There's one piece of advice I drill into the clients I work with. It's time tested, having held true since prehistoric men and women were drawing stories on cave walls. *If you want them to share, first you must make them care.*

New ways to deliver, engage with and share content

Social media is the most dynamic and complex media environment there ever was. Identifying audiences, scheduling events, cross-platform promoting, collaborating, listening, researching, re-targeting — all of this and more before you even start creating content.

But while the platforms are forever changing and tweaking their algorithms there is one element in the whole social media formula that remains unchanged.

Humans. And, in particular, the way the human brain absorbs and engages with content.

People and their behaviours around processing content remain much the same. While social media is often billed as the great disruptor, the truth is that human attention and what captures it hasn't evolved nearly as rapidly as the platforms themselves. The way our brains consume and process images, text and videos hasn't changed — only the way we access, deliver and share them.

Technology has changed how we access the things we have always and will always crave — stories, information, entertainment, news, art, drama, music... the list goes on. So the best way to manage the ever-changing digital landscape is to adopt a strategy that targets natural, instinctive human behaviours. The part of social media that people like Mark Zuckerberg can't change. As you will learn throughout this book, this is an evergreen, win–win approach. First, your audience craves content that is created the way their brain is designed to digest it, and the social media platforms crave and survive on content that delivers and holds people's attention.

Viral videos exist because the platforms have created an environment in which they thrive, where the content that triggers the greatest levels of engagement is rewarded. Before the emergence of social media, stories, scandals, jokes and gossip still spread and circulated through society; it just didn't happen so efficiently. People naturally, instinctively communicate with one another, as they always have. Now we've just developed more and better tools for doing so. The internet has put the rumour mill on steroids; one-to-one conversations have become one-to-thousands interactions.

The internet provides radically different ways for an audience to respond to content, triggering the platform to spread it further. The interactions we make still occur in the moment; what's different is the ease with which we can reach way more people than previously possible.

While the printing press, radio and TV increased audiences massively through their greater reach, the act of commenting on and sharing that information remained at a face-to-face, human-to-human, word-of-mouth level. Sharing a cave painting with others is necessarily restricted to your own immediate social group. Today's social media platforms, on the other hand, are built around interactions and engagement on a vast scale. 'The Facebook' started as a (rather sleazy) way for college students to share whether they thought one of their fellow students was 'hot or not'. Opinion that was usually reserved for locker rooms and parties enjoyed a cyber injection and spread across campuses at a frightening rate.

This layer of interaction on top of content, the ability for all to be involved, was clearly addictive. On Twitter everyone can have their say; on Facebook every moment can be celebrated; on Instagram every success can be posted. Our appetite for being a part of something bigger than ourselves, and for projecting an image of our life as better or fuller than others', feeds not only our egos but also our hunger for content. For platforms fighting to maintain greater levels of attention, content that draws a crowd is golden, and those creating it are rewarded.

In the early days of YouTube you could actually consume every video posted. That ceased to be possible a long time ago. For brands, the situation is flipped: posting content on social media is in itself no guarantee the audience you are targeting is ever going to get to see it. That's right. For all the uproar about being safe online and never posting things you wouldn't want to share in public, the truth is most content is only ever exposed to a tiny fraction of the people you hope will see, read and engage with it.

A viral video overrides the usual limits on reach and exposure, which is why understanding how to identify and implement content using your unique Viral DNA code is and will continue to be so powerful and important. I like to say that by empowering more people to make better content, we are actually saving the internet, one bad video at a time. This is my mission.

Identifying high-quality, relevant content is by far the greatest challenge for social platforms, closely followed by promoting the quality content to the right users, so we don't end up drowning in irrelevant posts and traffic. We all know how the final chapter reads when platforms fail to manage carefully what they serve up to their user base ... Myspace anyone?

The research I'll share with you in this book will help you tackle these challenges and massively boost the engagement levels of your content. The answer, essentially, is about creating content using the Spread Factor.

The power of social media lies in the ability to properly understand how it works and why people use it the way they do. The 'touchdown play' is to enter any social media ecosystem and tell a story in such a way that it becomes sought after, is easily validated, and generates a desire in people to share it and pass it on. To achieve this, you first have to understand what it means to operate natively and seamlessly where you are targeting — that is, to create and post your content according to the particular nuances of that platform and the behaviours of the people who use it. For example, Facebook and Twitter handle content in very different ways. If you were to post your Tweets as Facebook status updates, you would create a friction that would turn people away. By posting natively you will be able to better convey your message with little friction and fewer distractions for your audience.

You, the new viewer

Since 2015, TV viewing habits have changed dramatically because access to content has changed. Only a few years back the internet and mobile data were expensive to access; now they're affordable. Ads were the price you had to pay to watch a TV show; now they're avoidable. Technology has made content relatively easy and cheap to produce, and social media has opened the gates for anyone to build a following through broadcasting their message.

What this has meant is the consumer is no longer locked into only watching TV. Growing up before the internet, brands had me cornered. Between *Masters of the Universe*, *Hong Kong Phooey* and *Justice League* cartoons, my TV viewing was filled with sugary cereal ads and commercials for the latest Mattel toys. If you have kids, or know any, take half an hour out of your day to observe how and what they watch.

Watching how young human beings interact with content is the first step in building an understanding of what and why viewers Like, Comment, Share and Buy. Kids get frustrated by comic books and magazines because they don't offer video; even adults get frustrated when their phone rings because they are in the middle of consuming content, much as when your mum would call you to come empty the dishwasher right in the middle of your favourite show. As a kid I remember thinking, 'Are you kidding me? I've waited a whole week to watch this!' And just like that the opportunity was gone. Remember the days when you couldn't pause a TV show? How did we even survive?

If you don't have kids and don't know how viewing habits have changed, here's a couple of examples from my family.

I have two daughters, who are now 13 and 10. Ms 10 has her own iPad. She doesn't have any social media accounts. She watches videos on YouTube, where she searches for two distinct types of content: music videos and animal videos. Pretty standard stuff. What I find intriguing is the *way* she searches for them. First, she will search for the artists and songs she already knows — right now it's Katy Perry. When the video shows up in search she selects it and then immediately opens a new YouTube tab and searches for the next song or video she wants to watch. Once she finds it she selects it and immediately opens another tab, and she repeats this before heading back to the first tab she opened where she can watch the video with the pre-roll ads already finished. In this way she doesn't have to wait to skip the ads — she avoids them altogether, on every video. I didn't teach that to her; it's a solution she discovered for herself. That's some ninja ad-avoiding sh!t right there. If you have ever spent money on pre-roll YouTube ads or banners and they didn't quite deliver the results you were after, that may be why.

You may think this is smart — I personally think it's genius when I stop to consider how much of my life I've spent watching TV ads. But the way Ms 13 navigates her TV watching is equally mind-blowing. When she wants to watch TV she plans ahead. On weekend mornings she'll check the TV channels and find the one that has the best line-up of what she wants to watch. She selects that channel and instantly pauses it then leaves the room, has her breakfast and waits for her sister to wake up. All this takes about 20 minutes. By the time she's ready to watch some TV she has enough minutes banked to fast forward all the ads.

I'm sure the TV ad sales guys aren't talking about these early adopter behaviours in their agency pitches.

So what has all this got to do with viral videos? The answer is *attention* — how to get it, and how not to be ignored or evaded by ad-avoiding ninjas, because if there's a way to manage it they'll work it out.

Viral videos flip the equation; they change the game, because rather than chasing the audience for their attention, viral videos are themselves sought after and greatly in demand. They *want* you. It is one of the only sure-fire ways to reach, inspire and engage with an entire generation of Millennials and Gen Zees.

tip

The first thing to get your head around is that you don't have to pay as much as you used to to promote your message. In fact, if you create 'shareable' content with Viral DNA you won't have to pay for distribution at all.

But if you do have a budget and you want to increase the rate at which your message spreads, putting money on content that embodies the Viral DNA or Spread Factor will further extend your reach and influence.

But understand younger consumers today are more sensitive and less forgiving than any generation that preceded them. Generation X, even Baby Boomers, are beginning to become more attuned to where they are paying their attention. Because they are spoilt for choice, they won't tolerate a less-than-premium experience. Any hint of a sell when they thought they were tuning in to be entertained or informed, and boom — you're done.

The upside is the online environment has so many channels that there is absolutely a place or platform suited to exactly what you want. It's all down to you, your style and your audience. This is important, because what you produce has to be tailored to the differences and nuances of each particular platform. Whenever you think about investing in content you have to work through three questions: what do they want, when do they want it and in what form does it need to be delivered? Think about it. Anyone familiar with Instagram knows that a big part of its traditional attraction has been the endless stream of stylish and stunning photos. It's now moving towards video and live broadcasting, but using it in a very different way from YouTube and Facebook. So it's important to know where you stand in your audience's eyes because you need to be seen as offering a seamless fit, not as an opportunistic stranger just hanging around to sell stuff.

Then there's cost. It's the biggest headache for most businesses. What's this going to cost? And my answer remains the same. Your business. It's an unavoidable fact that if you stop marketing your business at the same time as your clients are consuming, you will lose. If you cease to be noticed because your audience is too busy looking at your competitors, you lose. If you fail to show up, you lose.

The answer is not to simply maintain a presence on social media but to create content that hijacks viewers' attention and triggers them to spread your message. Thanks to social media, the audience now wields incredible power. Not only can they choose what they watch and when they watch it, but they can also influence what others watch and the context in which they view it. Essentially, your business's existence depends on how your content is received. To adapt an old philosophical puzzle, if a business puts a video on YouTube and nobody watches, is it still a video?

This book isn't about either how to frame a selfie or how to manage large-scale video productions. The Virable formula is about how you build and shape your most potent brand story and tell it in the most compelling and contagious way possible. It's about how to identify and capture the ingredients of the most-watched videos on the planet.

You don't need big, expensive cameras or an army of production supervisors to create the types of videos that can influence the future of your business or bottom line. Sure, there are times when they'll help make things *look* better, more cinematic perhaps, but they'll rarely have a significant effect on the level of attention you capture, how long you can hold it or the response your message triggers.

recap:
NEW TOOLS STILL REQUIRE
OLD THINKING

- Social media is here to stay and it is only going to get bigger and more powerful.

- Social media success is based on existing, time-tested communication principles.

- Attention leads to Stimulation, which triggers an Action. Following those three steps will guarantee video cut-through on any budget.

strategy

Focus on the experience the next time you have an idea for a video, or even think of a post you may have recently made. If it was a sales video, did you speak only of the benefits and features of what you were trying to sell? Or maybe you were somewhere exotic, like a tropical paradise? Did you talk about how close the hotel is to the beach and reel off how many pools and bars it has?

If so, I suggest you focus more on the experience, how the product will make you feel, or how living in paradise has changed your mindset or outlook on life.

Let your viewer feel it.

chapter 3
sharing: a modern-day mystery

▶

Take a moment to think of all the major social media platforms of today. The big players. Your list will likely look much like this:

- ▶ Facebook
- ▶ Twitter
- ▶ Instagram
- ▶ YouTube
- ▶ LinkedIn
- ▶ Snapchat
- ▶ TikTok.

These are the most successful, populated platforms on the planet. All of them are very different, attracting users for different reasons, looking for different experiences. All of them have one common feature, a major function that sets them apart from those that have tried and failed.

Each of these platforms has successfully integrated and encouraged the ability to SHARE, whether it be your life story or content you consume and find interesting.

Share is the mayor

Sharing is the most important ingredient of success in the new media world, and the platforms that encourage it are not only already dominating but will continue to grow. If sharing wasn't as easy to do as it is, viral content wouldn't exist, selfies would only circulate among friends and humans would act very differently.

The ability to share, at scale, has changed the way we interact. Fans value a written autograph from a celebrity or sports star much less than a selfie with the star, because it can be shared way more easily to way more people.

Sharing is the most important action or response a brand or individual can seek on a social platform — it's a pathway to success. Having customers post a photo of themselves with a newly purchased product, along with a description about how pumped they are about it, is more important for a brand than having a potential customer find your website. Let me explain.

A potential customer who finds online content endorsing the quality of a product is more likely to buy it. Such peer validation helps influence our buying decisions. Facebook and Instagram know this, which is why they are introducing the functionality for customers to buy products directly from inside their platforms. Encouraging customers to share their excitement around a new purchase in real time has become a very powerful promotional proposition. Look at how Apple handle the release of a new iPhone. They set up a big scene at the point of sale in every store so when the proud new owner emerges from spending more than $1000 on an iPhone (when a lesser brand could do much the same thing for a fraction of the cost) they create a special moment for the customer. In that moment that customer is the centre of attention. At the time, those waiting, watching or merely walking past are drawn to the scene and some are persuaded that they too want to be one of the first to get one.

Sharing taps into another very important driver embedded deep in the human psyche. Ego.

In the new media world, it is very important for individuals, marketers and brands to understand what fuels the ego of their followings. Ego is a state of mind that when triggered will, in a split second, have someone sharing your story or content. Knowing what to include in your content or story is key to spreading your message. The internet is full of advice on the elements needed to trigger customer ego, including being relevant and intriguing, and making sure you deliver value. All of these elements play a role, although there is no one, single sweeping formula that provides the key to viral contagion for everyone. That's just not how it works. As groups and as individuals we are all different, with different lived experiences, different values, different needs and desires. Just as each one of us is genetically unique, every content creator needs to know how to express or broadcast their story with their own Viral DNA in mind.

On the upside, because we are all unique, there's an audience for almost everyone and everything. (Not convinced? Go to YouTube or Facebook, type in 'ASMR' and you'll soon understand what I mean.) Some viral videos spread because they earn those who share them bragging rights among their friends or peer circle. If as a brand you can help an individual earn points among their friends by helping them promote their position or hold onto a mantle, then they will be happy to buy your products or services. In fact, they will become a champion for your cause because spreading your message benefits them.

In my circle of friends, for example, this works around any content relating to the *Star Wars* movie franchise. I am the recognised

Star Wars source, so whenever any new source delivers great *Star Wars* content, I am going to join that community and will stay there as long as *Star Wars* talk retains currency in my community.

This is the essence of the formula: it is designed to generate an army of brand loyalists who will never leave, not only because they are indebted to you for the kudos you have helped them earn, but because they can't wait to share whatever it is you post next. If the content triggers the Like, Comment and Share actions, which in themselves act as peer validation for your brand, product or service, the natural next step is to Buy. But it's only after your viewers have connected so deeply as to trigger those actions that you should even consider a Sell.

Consider this. Say you are looking to take up golf. You've never played it before or had the slightest interest in it, but suddenly you feel inspired to play. The first thing you're going to have to do is buy a set of clubs. To make that purchase decision you'll most likely go one of two ways: you'll ask the advice of your golf-playing buddies or you'll conduct an independent online search.

One of the biggest influences on your decision will no doubt be price. But the next biggest influencer will be your peers. If when you search online you find reviews from experienced golfers, or even better new golfers, talking about how good the clubs have been for them, then you, my friend, are already well down the sales funnel. Viral videos by their very nature rank high in search results and as result are very influential.

In fact, online peer validation, reviews, posts and comments that reach the front page of Google, by being shared and engaged with, are the very first thing a brand should be looking to have show up when someone searches their name, product or service. Yep. Post a peer-validated video first. Then your website underneath it. That way your customer will be further along their purchase decision journey than if they landed directly on your website.

Out of all the actions people can take, sharing is the basis for success behind all social networks and anyone doing business on them.

So in social media town, Likes and Comments show progress, but Share is the mayor because it's the step before Buy. So what does this mean to brands, the new breed of broadcasters and how they should be creating their videos? It changes everything, because you aren't producing videos to reveal product specs and advantages; you're producing videos that trigger a viewer instinctively to Like, Comment and Share in order to bring them closer to Buying. (I'll teach you just how to do this later in the book.)

With greater volumes of content being produced than ever before, it's also important to understand how platforms like Facebook, YouTube and LinkedIn are coping with the overload, because the last thing you want is for your videos to be lost in the social media abyss. It may come as no surprise, but 99 per cent of all content uploaded to the internet is of no relevance to you, while a different 99 per cent is irrelevant to me. You may be interested in cooking, for instance, while I couldn't care less about it!

Without first capturing the attention of your key audience, you'll have no chance of triggering them to share.

The upper-level game

As a creator, how can you navigate this content dilemma so you achieve maximum cut-through with the videos you make? You have to understand intrinsically your position as a business, your brand, your message, and most importantly your audience and why they follow you. It almost sounds backwards when you have always made your videos on the back of what seemed like a 'good idea'.

So how do you avoid this?

Rule number one (and probably the mistake I see most often across businesses I help): don't make the video you want; make the video your audience is desperate to *share*. Why? Because social media networks will reward you for it. This is about playing the upper-level game. If you are simply focused on your view count or converting everyone to your way of thinking, you have already lost. You need to be attacking social media from an elevated view, especially if you plan to use it to attract business and awareness. Your greatest advantage comes from simply shifting your mindset from participating to understanding the main game and how you can play right into the hands of the platforms themselves.

Right now, platforms like Facebook, Instagram, Twitter and even YouTube are drowning in crap content. On Facebook, for example, first it was 'follow us for a free ice cream', coupon-type marketing that clogged up the newsfeed, then came 'follow these instructions for your chance to win an iPad'. In Facebook's defence they have moved to stamp out a lot of these tactics, but let's be clear: they didn't do it to save you, they did it to save themselves. If Facebook hadn't moved to shut down all the crappy spam posts and improve the newsfeed experience, their audience would have moved somewhere else.

By playing this hand, Facebook has clearly shown the pathway individuals and brands should follow if they want to keep being heard and present on the biggest social platform ever built. That pathway to success is paved by engagement. The number one media form for engagement is undoubtedly video. That means moving beyond content that interests you to what I describe as active audience content. Nothing else matters.

You only have to look at how Facebook ranks content. They use the term 'sessions' to describe interactions or engagement with content, and sessions are ranked as either positive, neutral or negative within the Facebook algorithm. Viewing a video is ranked as a neutral interaction — generally of no benefit. Commenting and sharing (physical actions) are ranked as positive interactions. The more sharing you can get your audience to do, the further both your audience and the algorithm will send your video.

tip

If a social media agency starts talking about how you must be posting at least three times a day, no matter what, I suggest you run the other way. The reason I say this is that this isn't a volume game. As a friend of mine who started a global sports brand used to say, 'The world doesn't need another marl grey t-shirt.' He's right, and the internet doesn't need any more boring sales videos.

Don't upload content just for the sake of keeping a streak running. You need to focus on producing content that triggers a response. That way you know whether or not it worked. Only once your content is attracting the responses you're hoping for should you think about increasing your production frequency, and even then only if you can do so while maintaining the same response rates.

I originally set out to find the 'one script fits all' to viral success that would play into the artificial intelligence that controls the algorithms and in turn the spread of content across social platforms. A formula I could duplicate for brands and businesses that would allow me to run a production company built around influencing human behaviours, monitoring trends and backing ourselves to own the attention of the internet, even just for a moment. Sadly, the one-size-fits-all approach doesn't work for this type of communication. What I did find though is a pattern, a sequence, a series of steps that all viral videos achieve.

You see, social media platforms can tweak their algorithms whenever they want ... and they frequently do. But what they can't mess with is what their audience wants. If the platforms start serving up videos that users don't want to watch, soon enough they won't have any users. So it's in their best interests to keep the masses engaged. The key is to focus on how people behave with content rather than trying to game the algorithms driving the individual platforms.

I believe this shift in thinking is a significant breakthrough in understanding the science behind successful viral content and video and being able to repeat it. YouTube is full of videos on how to gain 1000 Instagram followers overnight or 10 000 views on YouTube in a week, but I've yet to find one that isn't gaming the platform in some way. It's a short-term trick or a bug that leads to a rise in the vanity statistics but never the engagement levels.

Focusing on the human element is playing the long game. The shift, the key I spent years on, is understanding not simply what or who you are as a creator or business or brand, but what you are for your audience. And once you understand that shift, you start to understand that your success in this space begins to rely on how finely tuned you are to your own DNA — the code that attracted your audience to you to begin with.

Later in the book I'll share with you a process that will guide you to better isolating and understanding your own Viral DNA, to creating contagious content and having the ability to influence behaviour. But first I think it's important to better understand the background of viral videos better — where they come from, how they spread, and importantly what role the platforms themselves play in viral success or failure.

Viral videos — a short history

There's no doubt that the most high-profile examples of viral success have been spawned by YouTube. Other evolving platforms are starting to catch up, but YouTube blazed the trail and gave birth to this radically powerful online force. So why YouTube? What was it that made this platform the birthplace of viral videos?

The answer lies in their early belief in the power of sharing. While traditional media hoarded and protected their content and restricted where it could be consumed, YouTube went the other way. They zigged when the world was zagging. It's a story of disruption that has become almost commonplace online nowadays. Do things differently. YouTube's difference was allowing users to share the content they had found more easily. They didn't sweat about copyright issues (I'm sure they were doing all they could) and they embraced a user experience where the audience was given control over what attracted the most attention. In fact, the front page of YouTube became, and remains, a coveted position for any video as it guarantees hundreds and thousands, if not millions, of views.

The key was that YouTube included Share buttons on their interface, and not just one or two; in all, there are 17 ways to share a video from YouTube. This is not only a marked advantage that social platforms have over traditional media, but also an advantage YouTube held over other social platforms in its formative years. Even in the very early days, YouTube pioneered the sharing of videos by making it possible to send links via email. It sounds no more than common sense nowadays, but not that many years back it wasn't a viable option. YouTube links and email allowed people to satisfy the desire to share without having to carry all the information contained in the video in the body of the email; it was the bypass needed to avoid the wrath of that pesky mailerdaemon, which would block big files from travelling the email networks.

So viral videos were born — and became the holy grail of marketing. They attract attention and foster engagement, which is what makes them viral. When they spread, they carry the validation of peers, and of course their distribution is free.

Brand videos fit the viral mould perfectly. They aren't based on luck; they're engineered according to a formula that in its most basic form grabs your attention, gets you emotionally connected and triggers you to take action. As long as it's easy for all three of these elements to play out, then the content will spread.

We know the major social networks are driven by algorithms. These algorithms are fed information from actions; content is valued based on those actions. And the data tentacles have a deep reach. If someone watches/reads, shares, likes or comments on your content, the search algorithms take note of it. If the people you shared it to consume the content or Share, Comment and Like, then your content will be rated more highly. The more of these validations your content can trigger, the sooner and more freely it will rise to the top.

Each platform works in different ways. They may change the weight they put on certain elements or engagements, but in the end it's the actions they promote most that will deliver the greatest reward.

On YouTube many years ago, securing 10 000 views within 7 to 10 days would earn you a place on the front page of the site, and 30 per cent of visitors would watch every video on the front page. As a result, any videos that made it to the front page racked up even more views through the added exposure. The front page of your YouTube experience is now influenced by your behaviours, subscriptions and search data. The 'Trending' page comes closest to resembling the old home page. The significant difference is that it's a mixture of algorithm-generated channels and videos as well as some 'internal', human-influenced selections, such as channels or videos that are blowing up or they just seem to like. YouTube also features data such as watch time, your rating as an engaged community member and how many people you have triggered to start watching a video on the platform.

Facebook is slightly different, as viewing is assessed as a passive indicator. At the time of writing, the Facebook algorithm more resembles a gated community. When you post content, only a fraction of your follows are exposed to it; this is called organic reach. Essentially, they are the guinea pigs who decide the fate of your content. If they engage with it, then Facebook will open the gates for others to engage with it too. So as long as people keep engaging your content will keep spreading. The downside is if you post content at a time when the guinea pigs aren't around or the random selection includes sleeper or fake accounts that you paid to earn overnight, then your content, no matter how good it is, is doomed.

One way to ensure it is seen is to spend some advertising dollars to promote it and get it started, then let its viral nature take over. Now before you jump on me, Facebook remains the most cost-effective ad platform around, and if your content is as good as it should be by the time you get to the end of this book, you won't be spending much to make sure it gets started (and you shouldn't have bought those fake followers to begin with).

An additional area to be aware of with Facebook is the rise of dead or dormant followers. While I recommend you only ever post engaging content, don't get relaxed and leave it too long either. Wired into Facebook's algorithm is the effective equivalent of a black hole. The way this works is that if you are lucky enough to be served content as a chosen follower and you don't respond or engage with the content or you don't interact with the associated person's or brand's page or newsfeed, then Facebook will start leaving you out of the loop, meaning you won't be chosen as a sample account and you won't be served content from those people or pages, even if you follow them.

Engaging with the content or searching for the brand or page will put you back on the radar, but with so much information flooding through the Facebook feed it's easier than ever to be forgotten. And if you are struggling to get traction or attention with content you are convinced is premium (now really be aware and check again if it truly is premium), then one reason Facebook isn't working for you could be that your account has been turned down on your audience. This could be for a number of reasons but being of 'good standing' and having a positive report card associated with your profile is important to Facebook. The more you operate outside their guidelines, the less people will see of you. Equally, the less engaging your content becomes, the more hidden from the newsfeeds you will become. If your content sucks, expect to be sucked into the dark blue Facebook abyss of irrelevance.

From the platform side, to keep us coming back Facebook, YouTube, Instagram and others have created reward systems that don't discriminate based on whether you have spent a fortune on production or use a studio. The only measure by which social platforms favour some content over other content is *engagement*, and the highest-ranking engagement tool, the one that brings the most reward, is the Share button. The reason for this weighted approach is simple: great content keeps people on the platform longer. The more shares a piece of content attracts, the more times it has been validated by a viewer as valuable. As a result, the platforms are motivated to introduce the 'valuable' content to new viewers with every click of the button. This makes the platform itself more valuable as brands line up to take advantage of the highly segmented audience sample that can clearly demonstrate skyrocketing levels of real human attention.

This is why brands and social media platforms love sharing, but what about consumers? Why are we so interested in what other people deem to be interesting?

From a psychological perspective, content distributed as a friendly 'Share', human to human, from a friend or someone you follow or admire, rather than via a paid or pushed method, removes the negativity of the hard sell. Your instinctive defences that protect you from being sold to or wasting your time are lowered. In your mind, your friends who shared the content have not only deemed it safe to watch but have flagged it as something you *should* see. They have taken the risk and given it the thumbs up, which has introduced a second influence: the fear of missing out or, as the woke generation say, #FOMO. No one wants to be out of the loop, so if something is spreading like wildfire and fuelling the conversations in your social circle, you don't want to be the one who has no idea what everyone is talking about. It's a brutal reality but one we all have to live with, because it's driven by our instincts and ego. Social media has introduced a competitive need to be continually informed, to be in the know rather than out in the dark.

recap:
THE SHARE MARKET

- Sharing validates your content — and in turn your brand, service and product.

- Understand the characteristics and nuances of each platform and tailor your content for best fit.

strategy

At the time of writing, Facebook faced a massive dilemma: a glut of 'low-value' ads. Businesses, brands and individuals spending $10 a week to keep eyeballs on a post they put together poorly. In the meantime, big brands are only dipping their toes in, slowly shifting their spend to the social network.

There are so many of these low-rate ads in the Facebook system that they simply don't have enough content in the newsfeed to serve them. And Facebook don't want to burn the low-end media buyers because they are the foundation of the platform itself.

The answer is your opportunity. Facebook needs more enriched content to serve ads on. That means video that attracts responses, not just views. Upload contagious content, particularly live streams, because they drive more comments, and Facebook will thank you for helping them out of a jam by rewarding you with more reach.

chapter 4
context: pixels with purpose

▶

If your audience doesn't know where you're coming from when you communicate, then there is no chance they can tell whether or not the information is relevant to them. The way I like to look at it is this: if you don't know where you stand, how do you know which story to tell or how to tell it.

This is the importance of context.

Context is built, shaped and communicated in so many ways — from what you've said in the past to what you say now, from how you look to the country you live in, from how much money you have to how much you say you have, the look and feel of your brand, the platforms you populate, the clothes you wear or don't wear ... the list goes on. Almost anything can influence your context or the context in which you are communicating. It has an integral impact on your content and can be best thought of as a form of assumed knowledge in the audience before they even click play on your videos.

Message clarity and consistency

Viral videos pop because they have a consistent context across *all* the content created under that brand banner. I know of brands that have worked on posting videos for months to establish context around their channel before dropping the main video that they engineered to go viral.

This contextualising is about priming your audience for what is coming next, but you need to understand that one out-of-context post in the months leading up to the big launch can be all it takes to do serious damage. Social platforms are always measuring and ranking you, which can explain inconsistencies in views and interactions between different videos posted to the same channels. This is why it is vital that you remain consistent in your positioning.

With an overcrowded, noisy social media ecosystem, people are more tempted to cheat the system, to find a short cut to success. Social media platforms are wise to this, and no black hat methods last long anymore. There's only one truly rewarding way to cut through and stand out from the crowd and that is with absolute clarity around your message. The magic ingredient that most people miss is *context*. You can provide all the content in the world but if it isn't relevant, and isn't delivered in a form that your target audience expects, then you have already lost, no matter how good it is.

Context is so powerful that if you get it right, audiences will actually forgive deficiencies in other areas. That's why a low-budget video with shaky camera work and bad audio can still be a huge success. If the information or experience is so deeply relevant to the context of a problem or a need someone has, then nothing else actually matters. The audience will lock into what you have to offer, ignoring the technical shortcomings. Of course you want to deliver the best quality you can at all times, but the message always outweighs the window dressing.

Think of all those videos of kids jumping off roofs, crashing through trampolines or stacking their bikes. The quality of the video work usually isn't that great, the shots are bumpy, the audio is noisy and scratchy. If you came upon it on TV, you'd probably reach straight for the remote. Watch these same videos on the internet, and you understand the context is different: the conditions under which they were captured were quite different; they weren't professionally staged, they were real, authentic, so you accept their flaws.

YouTube stars attract millions of views to every video they post. These videos may be filmed in a bedroom or shed, and this context can actually add to their attraction. They are more engaging partly because the viewers may also be sitting in their bedrooms leaning over their laptop or phone. This presents these stars with a challenge. As their popularity rises and they start making serious cash, they will be tempted to raise the production quality of their videos, maybe move their operation to a studio, seek a TV deal, add fancy effects. Such changes are often all it takes to drive their content out of context to a point where they will eventually disconnect from their audience.

On the flip side, the internet itself, the platforms and even our viewing habits, are all constantly evolving, so staying the same isn't an option either. It is easy to feel like there are all these moving parts and somehow you need to navigate them all perfectly. There is one way to get it right more often than not, and that is to truly understand your audience and the context in which they access your content. Having this knowledge will allow you as a creator to evolve with them, to grow, adjust and mature as they do, to adjust your look, feel and the context to what is most relevant to them at the time. Truly mastering this art is the difference between an overnight success that disappears just as quickly and a long-term trusted source.

One of the biggest challenges around context is that many people fail to understand what it actually is, and that's easily done because it's such a variable. Context is by its nature subjective because we are all wired differently.

Context is the information that forms the setting around information, an event or an idea and gives it meaning. It's the understanding our brain forms based on all the information we have at our disposal, including our life experience, to make an assessment of what we believe is happening.

For example, say you are listening to just the audio of a video, you can't see the screen. In the audio is a woman — let's call her Karen — and she is yelling, 'I hate you Rickey, arrghh! That's it. I'm done.'

Picture in your head right now the woman yelling these words, the look on her face, her evident rage. What do you imagine Ricky did? Something seriously bad, right? Now, what if I added some context? Could I change your perceptions of the scene? Of course I could. Further information can be very influential in shaping what our hearts and minds perceive. Maybe Ricky had just poured talcum powder in her hair dryer? And what we're hearing is Karen's immediate response when she turns it on.

It's a (very unwelcome) prank. So, maybe divorce isn't on the cards. Maybe Ricky has escaped jail time, for now.

The point I want to drive home is that the surrounding circumstances in which your content is consumed (its context) are incredibly important, and the creators of viral videos pay particular attention to this. Remember they aren't the product of luck; they are meticulously planned and executed.

In social media terms, context is the greater knowledge or assumed learnings about an individual, brand or business — about *your* brand or business if you are creating the video. You need to decide:

- ▶ what story to tell
- ▶ where to tell it
- ▶ and exactly how it needs to be told.

This means not only the nature of the story itself and your role in it, and its audience, but the format and the manner in which it is produced. The style and feel of your content adds context for your audience, giving them an idea of what they can expect with the next video. This is a massive challenge for YouTubers who are now using the platform to go live. Live streaming is a powerful tool. Among many other things, it delivers an authentic insight into the minds and personalities of the people on the stream. If you are an expert, there is no better way to prove this than to do so live. But at the time of writing many YouTubers were experiencing declines in their subscription numbers every time they launched a stream. Why? It's hard to be certain, but from my observations the livestream content is being delivered in a different context from the original content that first persuaded the audience to take action and subscribe. The connection with your audience is so brittle that all these things truly matter.

Three common fails

Here are three common fails to avoid when it comes to context. (In Part II you'll learn exactly how to create the best context around your messaging.)

1. Know your hunting ground

You need to know what you're doing. The quickest way to undo all your good video work is to post content that doesn't fit the natural environment of the platform you're posting to. Every social platform has nuances and quirks that drew in the crowd to begin with.

The most common mistake by brands and individuals is to cross-post the same content between different platforms. They do it because the option is available and it's easy to do, but the audiences are vastly different and the same post will rarely work well on both.

By not taking account of the nature of the platform and why people are paying massive amounts of attention to it, by remaining ignorant of its ecosystem, those posting 'out of context' work are quickly assessed as out of touch or uncool, and followers will abandon them in droves.

2. Match your brand to your production level

In another classic context fail, brands in particular try to get sneaky. There's a common trend to use hidden cameras to catch the spontaneous reactions of unsuspecting witnesses of extreme pranks and stunts. Part of the attraction for viewers is certainly voyeuristic, part is 'being in on the joke'. But here's where major brands often fail. The videos that make up the majority of this category can be traced back to dorm room or university/college humour. A lot of these videos are captured on phones hidden on bookshelves. From a production perspective they are far from perfect but it's the context that makes them gold. They are real and authentic, and the fact that we know they aren't rehearsed or fake makes the reactions even more precious.

Big brands that try to be cool in this space don't always fake the reactions but they do, almost always, overproduce the content. I suspect that because brands pay big dollars for video content, the video producers feel obliged to use high-end professional equipment and technicians to deliver the final product. To the 'dialled in' modern consumer who is instinctively equipped with ninja-like abilities to sense the fake, an overproduced video triggers an instant mental resistance against the sell that must inevitably follow to pay for those high-end production values.

So what happens? Well, the audience tunes out; they abort and abandon any plans to engage or share. So when you are making videos you need your production values to match the context in which you are delivering your message. If you are a budget lawn-mowing brand and lowest price is your point of difference, then a five-camera 4K definition production probably isn't going to match the context in which you tell your story. It would be way more effective for you simply to record your videos on your phone... maybe from the back of your ride-on mower.

3. Don't forget they're human, and so are you

Beyond the nuances of each individual platform, truly knowing your context means understanding your audience and forming a relationship with them. As with any other human relationship, it all begins with listening. Listen hard and you'll begin to build an understanding of what your audience wants, when they want it and in what form. The better you know them, the clearer the creative direction of your content will become and the greater the advantage you can derive by continually delivering videos that are so dialled into your followers' lives they'll suspect you've been listening to them talk in their sleep.

These three steps all shape the context of your videos.

The platforms themselves also add context to content. It amazes me how many brands and individuals ignore the characteristics of popular platforms. Each of them has a unique angle or advantage that the others don't have, and your content should be tailored to take advantage of those differences. The way I approach different social platforms is similar to how I approach marketing myself in different countries. If you don't speak their language, you're never going to generate much interest.

Understanding context

When we're talking about viral content, the most popular content on the planet, it's a given that a populated platform helped the journey. It goes without saying that YouTube played a massive role in creating a better way for viral videos to attract more views. Sure, viral videos had been around before YouTube, but it was a complicated process that was severely constrained by the size of the files that could be attached to an email, and to get people sharing recipients had to be fully engaged. I remember times when I would be sent a video to watch via email and I would give up scrolling to the bottom of the email to watch the video because it had been forwarded so many times.

Today the process is comparatively frictionless and it continues to evolve towards the point where the videos you want to watch and share will *find you*.

The most popular platforms became that way for a reason. They understood how users wanted to experience content and also that they wanted a place where they could interact and engage with each other. The world has already done half the work for you: people have filtered out the inferior social networks and rewarded the videos that attract the most attention, and the platforms use web crawlers and cookies to help them serve your videos to people who want to watch or have an interest in your category.

Context is the first hurdle to clear when creating viral content, so you need to immerse yourself in the world where those who you want to communicate with live and learn what drives them. Take note of the content they share, its context and the responses it draws in the comments. Focusing on the environment will enhance your own understanding of the context.

A story involving the American fast-food giant Arby's offers a good illustration. Arby's had a deal with Pepsi and in the hustle and bustle of business they forgot to hold up their end of the bargain. Of course, Pepsi weren't happy. What followed was a great example of understanding and utilising context to your advantage.

Arby's knew that their everyday customers wouldn't care that they had failed to meet an obligation in a complex business arrangement, but they also knew that in the world of business media anything involving a giant like Pepsi was going to draw attention, and that attention would then reverberate through the blog networks and online channels. So rather than prepare a standard apologetic press release that would be alluded to briefly in the last paragraph of a story in which the journalist had already torn shreds off the company, Arby's attacked the issue with a viral mindset, using the mistake to drive publicity and connect closer with their ordinary customer. By being fully attuned to current consumption habits they used the error to engineer a viral video. The team at Arby's took a less than flattering situation and made themselves the heroes of the hour, winning an army of new fans. The reporting, both online and in the mainstream media, on Arby's big stuff-up with Pepsi focused more on the clever use of social media than the potentially brand-damaging mistake they'd made. The result? The publicity from the video created the type of exposure money can't buy — for both Pepsi and Arby's.

Gary Vaynerchuk argues persuasively that 'Content is King', but he also suggests that 'Context is God'. Facebook expert Mari Smith agrees that Content is King but argues that '"Engagement is Queen"... and she rules the house.'

Content, Context, Engagement... What do I think? I think we need them all. I believe that the era of simply making videos is over and that now creators have to get smarter. More strategic. While the audience evolves, so do the creators. We need all three, because none will survive for long without the others. Viral videos enjoy high levels of all three.

The context of viral videos is so clear that there is no mistaking where the storytelling is coming from. I would argue the viewers whose actions fuel most viral videos have an assumed knowledge about the creator or brand even before they watch the video. They are already buying into what is on offer.

Viral videos are of course content, but more and more they are surrounded by 'supporting' content. The ecosystem has evolved past the one outstanding video that takes the world by storm. Sure, they still happen, but they don't happen anywhere near as often. Viral videos tend to be launched off the back of previous content that has already primed an audience and established the context.

Finally there's engagement. If viral videos are skyrockets, engagement is the rocket fuel. Engagement drives the reach and spread. Without an assumed knowledge around the context no one is going to risk wasting their time to watch something that may be irrelevant to them.

So rather than arguing over which is more important, I prefer: 'Content is Currency.' Get it right and in today's environment content truly is as good as money. It brings attention, popularity, influence, exposure, trust and ultimately transactions. The fastest track to take if you are chasing all of the above is to understand your Viral DNA. Knowing where you stand and why your audience chose your message over your competitors'.

So what does context do and why is it important to grasp and understand? Context is an identifier. It is the values and beliefs that you hold and then project out into the world. It allows audiences to align with you or respectfully pass. And that brings us to a really important point.

If you make content for everyone you will end up with an audience of no one. It's a massive fail to try to please the whole world.

As an online brand you want to build a territory, or what some call a 'tribe'. By building a territory, you are creating a space to accommodate like-minded people. You are saying, this is what we stand for, this is our shared belief. If you feel the same, come over here and be part of our community. These shared beliefs and understandings give context to the issues and topics you communicate. If you have a 'tribe' of believers, they will play a major role in growing your audience, spreading your message and referring business your way.

Community first

Creating content simply to have a presence online, and producing articles, posts or videos to populate your site, is a time-consuming and often expensive journey, so if you develop content that doesn't connect, you are simply tearing up hundred-dollar bills. The surest pathway to connecting with your audience is ensuring you understand the context around what brought your audience together. If you want to trigger a response from them to your creative endeavours, you first need to understand what makes them tick. Why are they following you? What are they here for?

The easiest way to establish this is to develop clear beliefs that define what you stand for. While this sounds like some branding BS, when it comes to videos, TV shows or even movies, it is vitally important for achieving cut-through. Only once you know where you stand can you develop content that falls consistently within your brand boundaries and will deliver ongoing relevance and context to a reactive audience.

In social media marketing circles, having a tribe is much more powerful than having a following. A large following may be good for your ego, but it will do nothing for your business or cause if all they do is passively consume your content without engagement. In fact, based on how Facebook ranks content, passive viewers will hurt your reach and growth. Tribes engage; they will fight to defend what you and they believe in. Political parties build tribes. Religions build tribes. Brands and individuals need to build tribes too. Red Bull is a tribe. Whether we realise it or not, the way social media algorithms bring value to advertisers is by grouping us all into tribes. If you are marketing to these groups, their beliefs influence the context of the content, which drives engagement. You must feed your tribe from a menu that they set; your content is a freshly made dish they desire, and right now videos are hotter than tacos. If you get it right, your tribe will grow and flourish, and they will tell others how good it is and will invite them in, and soon you'll have a thriving community of like-minded individuals following your every post.

So to ensure your content is relevant, enabling you to make a deep connection, it is important to have a strong brand and a keen understanding of not only what your brand stands for but what your audience understands it to stand for.

Red Bull offers a great case study of context over content. The number one energy drink on the planet clearly knew where it was positioning itself as an early adopter of content marketing by establishing Red Bull Media House. Their move into this space is the reason they have delivered more views online than any other brand, with a stable of viral hits. In fact, Red Bull has been so successful that other long-established brands now have Red

Bull creating their media content for them, so 'the Bull' is now a broadcaster and production house. While Red Bull still plays in traditional advertising spaces with TV commercials, billboards and sponsorships, their commitment to online viral content means they are recognised as alpha disruptors in the broadcast space too.

Red Bull is recognised equally as an energy drink and as a purveyor of action sports videos, stunts and livestream broadcasts. You might even credit them with making mobile phones the primary device used by Millennials for consuming action sports content. With the money they have spent on video production and assets, Red Bull could easily have bought a TV licence, but they were acutely aware that producing content for lounge rooms across the globe was actually 'out of context' with how their audience wants to consume content. Their audience isn't inside watching TV, or when they are at home they are playing video games. 'Red Bull gives you wings' doesn't translate into sitting on the couch eating chips. It's a mantra or motto that conjures up a love of pushing boundaries, testing yourself, living life on the edge, so this is the context they develop, and they package their content in a way that lives up to the context we all now associate with the Red Bull brand.

Red Bull's success is based on the fact that their context fits 100 per cent with their brand. They have helped build and now own an entire genre — action sports. You know what you are going to get every time someone tags you on a Red Bull video, whether it's fast cars, mad men on motorbikes or crazy skiers on unrideable slopes. The point is you already have an assumed knowledge of the context, the territory you are entering or avoiding.

Rarely do any of these videos mention or show a can of the energy drink. Red Bull are conjuring up a lifestyle and continually providing their audience with value through videos they can't easily access anywhere else. It's the long game, so when the purchase decision arrives on the way to the local skate park, the decision is an easy one. 'Who has provided me with the most value in my life?' or 'Who am I indebted to?' or 'Who is aligned with my way of living and what I believe in?' Oh that's right, Red Bull gave me two hours of crazy viewing pleasure this week. I'll buy one of those. These are Millennials who experience zero TV screen time but are consuming more content than any generation before them. They are never detached from their mobile devices and they consume everything on demand — what they want, when they want it. Those moments are often when they are engaging with their extreme sport-loving friends, a perfect opportunity for the latest stunt to come into a conversation and for Red Bull to land some exposure as their content is delivered right into the conversation.

This scenario is exactly where marketing with content currently sits. The power has shifted away from brands and into the hands of independent humans armed with sophisticated devices. Marketers, in turn, have responded by creating an abundance of content that, for the first time, has to compete for the attention of the consumer with consumer-generated content.

Let's explore this for a second, keeping context in mind (warning: potential mind explosion moment). *The success of a video relies not on expensive cameras or professional edits but on relevance, authenticity and a defining context that triggers people to act.*

Let's go back to the skate park for a second ... If you are targeting the skateboarding kids, you have to be equal if not better at making the content they want to consume than they are. You have to be more relevant than a kid wanting to watch themselves. See how far you get if you try doing that from enemy territory or without a deep understanding of what makes them tick.

Add to the equation the understanding that the eighties are over and you can't spend your way to success anymore. Consumers are way too savvy and busy to waste time watching stuff they don't care about. It won't matter how many times you serve it up in their newsfeed ... if it's not for them, it's not for them.

The key to cutting through is using context to spark an interest, a connection in your audience. One that is developed off the back of deep insights.

And when you break through, the brain science that drives actions — Likes, Comments and Sharing — will push your content further than ever before. Sharing means your content is first sampled by someone else, who then recommends others try it too, much like the servants who had to test the King's dinner before he would in case it was poisoned.

If you don't have a 'food taster' handy, well, it's human nature that we are more likely to watch a video with a high rate of 'vanity' statistics than one that doesn't. If you are presented with two videos with the same thumbnail but one has two million views and the other only 200, you are more likely to watch the one with more views. Why? Because your time is precious and you don't want to waste it watching bad videos, and two million suggests strongly that this one is the safer bet.

recap:
THE FOUNDATIONS OF CONTEXT: CONTENT IS CURRENCY, BUT CONTEXT MAKES IT VALUABLE

- Know your hunting ground. Social platforms are sophisticated data analysts. They know if your videos have already played somewhere else or if your content or style doesn't align with the type of content that works for the audience they are catering for.

- Match your brand to your production level. Don't be afraid to publish videos with lower production values if that best suits the context of your brand or message.

- Listen. Listening to your audience, responding to them and interacting with them is the best way to understand them. Sadly, too many people post the videos they want to make rather than the videos their potential customers want.

exercise:
CLARIFYING YOUR CONTEXT

Context, at times, can be tricky to nail down, especially if you don't have a strong established brand or following or you have a history of posting schizophrenic content in order to attract more views.

Repetitive, consistent behaviour will help establish the context of your content faster than anything else you do. Context starts with *who you are*. It is influenced heavily by *who you are for your audience (or buyers)*. Success (or failure) depends on the strength of the values you share.

Later in the book I will work with you to establish real clarity around your context, but for that work to be effective we first need to establish a base or foundations from which to measure or grow.

This process will work better throughout the book if you choose one narrative to work on. If you are an entrepreneur with multiple ventures and looking to build your personal profile you may want to focus on 'You' as your brand. Alternatively, you may want to focus on a company. Whichever, choose one for the first pass. After your first complete read, feel free to follow this process again with different brands or subjects in mind.

Based on your current content catalogue (the posts you are putting out there):

Who are you? (Define your brand, in 25 words or less.)

_____

_____

_____

_____

Now imagine your viewing audience (real people you know only through a connection made through your content) and divide them into concentric circles, like a target.

Let's start with the bull's-eye 'Engaged' circle — the main targets.

These are viewers who not only watch but take action (Liking, Commenting, Sharing or Buying).

Who are your engaged viewers?

_____

_____

What drives them?

_____

_____

One circle further out are a group who watch your content but don't Like, Comment, Share or Buy. We call these 'Curious' viewers. They have made a minor commitment by watching, but for some reason the connection they make doesn't stimulate them enough to act.

Who are your curious viewers?

_____

_____

What is stopping them from becoming engaged?

_____

_____

And finally, the 'Disengaged' viewers in the outer circle. These are potential viewers who either have you in their feeds or the social media platform has put a sample of your content in front of them but they don't stop to engage.

I have a motto, a spin on an old marketing saying but it holds true of video production: 'Making videos for everyone is the fast track to building an audience of no one.'

Acknowledge three types of people your videos aren't made for. It's useful to define what makes a target viewer and what doesn't. For example, this book wasn't written for people who refuse even to try to make video a part of their marketing mix.

Let's call them 'video deniers'.

1. _____

2. _____

3. _____

Now you've made that list, you never have to worry about them again. But keep the rest of your work handy for some exercises later in this book.

chapter 5
likes, comments, action

The first chapters have focused on establishing common ground, and understanding how the world of *connection* and *communication* has been changed by the emergence of social media and the phenomenon of viral content. Because the world has changed, you have to change too if you want your business to survive, let alone thrive.

So how do you do it?

My single-minded focus when developing the Virable formula was to deliver an easy-to-follow process that would allow people like you to create the most contagious content possible, irrespective of your equipment or camera skills. In a way, I'd love the success of a video to be based purely on budget — it would certainly make production budget meetings with my clients a lot easier — but the reality is that a generous budget is not a guaranteed path to success.

The videos that cut through are more often than not those that protect and enhance everything that is unique and special about individual creators and businesses. What I'm saying is there are no cookie-cutter solutions here. Your story is yours to tell, and you are the best person to tell it. You have to not only maintain your identity but actively defend it from the fakes, impersonators and imposters.

'Do you' (*Be yourself*) is a favourite quote of mine, and it applies to your content too. Don't get romanced by others' success. Be open to learning but not desperate enough to copy; the world today is a small stage and you will get called out.

The Virable formula is geared to making your content contagious without compromising your unique values and traits. Any other approach won't stand the test of time, because you'll soon tire of keeping up appearances.

Applying the formula, the Spread Factor rates the 'shareability' of content. The higher the Spread Factor in your content the more likely it will go viral, drive engagement and make better connections, and deliver your audience closer to a purchasing decision. This calculation forms the basis for the most optimised approach to creating relevant, engaging content that is always in context.

Drawing on decades of production experience, and years of research into human behaviour and analysis of the world's most successful viral videos, the Spread Factor idea influences not only the way you need to be thinking but also your approach to content, marketing and strategy.

The system I have developed and tested is based on behaviours around video content. This focus is vital because video content is the main game, but it also works across all forms of media and communications. The lessons outlined in this book can be deployed to engineer more contagious speeches, emails, articles ... in fact, any form of communication can benefit.

As a journalist I was trained in how to identify the five elements needed to create a story: *characters*, *setting*, *conflict*, *resolution* and *lesson*. These are the minimum components required for a story to fly. Sometimes you might begin with only one of the five elements, and you'd have to get really busy to uncover the others and deliver your story by the deadline. Sure, sometimes story elements didn't make the cut, and the power in that situation was in understanding when to surrender and move on to the next one. By fully understanding the elements set out in this book, you'll be able to make those decisions in a split second. This is a skill that will not only save you time and money, but will enrich your content catalogue and as a result raise your ranking position according to the social platform algorithms.

In the new media world, deadlines for content aren't as cut-throat as they are in the news game. That's because viewing habits have changed so radically. The new technology allows consumers to access more of what they want when and pretty much wherever they want it. For the creator or producer, this lack of deadline is both a blessing and a curse. It means you can deliver content when it suits you with little or no penalty — that's the blessing. The curse is that so many stories are being published or posted that shouldn't make the cut. As a result, the social media world has become a very noisy place but also a space where potential viewers are very much on their guard for bad content. That means you have to work harder to win their trust.

Easily the most important lesson in this book, the lesson that will help you grow your audience and following faster than anything else, is in learning what it takes to produce an engaging story. There are certain elements that combine to make a story great, and you need to become so intimately familiar with them that you can make a judgement call on any creative concept in a moment.

My very first job, at a TV station, was a very interesting one, despite how it might sound. 'Commercial Inventory Manager' revolved around the split-second decisions viewers make when confronted with content. I was employed by Australia's Channel 9 to watch every advertisement/commercial and approve them to go to air. Now, this was the nineties when home shopping networks and after-midnight advertorials were all the rage. For two years I watched every commercial. Can you imagine what watching more than 8000 hours of TV commercials does to you? It makes you very sensitive to the annoying ones and very appreciative of those that aren't, and also hyper-aware that at the start, from the first frame, we viewers make a split-second decision on whether to tune in or tune right out.

I found this fascinating at the time, and still do, because it's a phenomenon that continues to apply today to both TV ads and online content. But even in my early media days I was fascinated by what made some ads attractive and others repellent. I started to follow the discussions among my friends closely. Knowing what my weekly work life involved, it never took long for my friends to turn any conversation into a discussion about TV advertising. There was usually some early chatter about the really 'bad' ones, though never any mention of the boring corporate ones. The conversation then always turned to the most memorable ones. This is a pattern I still see today, some two decades later.

The ingredient that differentiates them? STORY.

The power of story

Story is one of five key planks that influence the Spread Factor, the others being *brand story clarity, rules of engagement, emotional contagion* and *triggers*. Story has a very special role in the Virable formula because it's linked to instinctive behaviour in the human brain. If you shape your stories the way the human brain wants, then the connection between the viewer and the story is reinforced. This reinforced focus helps reduce distractions. Understand this in the context of the current environment, in which the world has never been so noisy, and you have a powerful advantage at your disposal. We are addicted to mobile devices that pummel us with messaging and images. We watch TV, eat meals, talk with friends, attend weddings and even funerals — all the while scanning our phones. If you want traction, you need to do more than just win attention; you have to maintain it, which is why the rules of storytelling, as outlined in chapter 9, are so important.

The Virable formula and understanding the concept of the Spread Factor help simplify the process of creating contagious video content. While most people are focused on how they look or what camera they need, Virable dives deeper. You already know you need to be creating content, but few gurus will teach you how to make the right content for you. It's time to focus on how to package the information delivered into the camera so it has the greatest chance of success — no matter how you look.

In a newsroom environment — and let's face it, this space is among the most prolific content creators on Earth — journalists need to know instinctively where the story they are working on fits. That is, not only which program but where in the show or section of the paper or website it will sit best. This is important because all these things influence how the piece will be produced — the pictures, the words, the learning, the journey and the value.

Newsrooms use rundowns to prioritise the content coming into them; it's a schedule based on *newsworthiness* — that is, what's going to attract and hold the largest audience. And over the past four decades on TV the art has been perfected to the point where viewer numbers would grow as the show played out. Set rundowns determine the relative importance of stories according to how much they affect their viewers' daily lives or how well the stories or images capture their attention and stop them from reaching for the remote. TV programming in general applies a similar system: the type of show you make determines when and where on TV it runs throughout the day or week.

It's this principle I want to teach you, because it will transform you from being simply a content creator who posts more or less randomly to a broadcaster who sets an audience up for a truly memorable experience. It is a magical distinction but is very rarely discussed. You may be saying to yourself, 'I don't want to learn about TV, I want to learn about YouTube and viral videos.' But you need to remember that the internet is the new version of TV and that the best lessons can be learned from the mistakes of those who have gone before you. TV has spent five decades making multi-billions of dollars capturing and holding the attention of billions of viewers, so of course it has many valuable lessons to teach us. And video storytelling, the online gold mine, happens to be a space in which TV has many years of expertise for us to draw on.

Right now, you and brands need to be thinking the same way TV stations think about their audience. You need to be looking, learning and adopting the broadcast model. As Gary Vaynerchuk warns us, if you aren't starting to operate like a media company then the risk is you won't have a business moving forward. But that is only half the model, because TV wasn't built for two-way communication. A TV audience is passive, TV ratings are at best estimates. Social media has changed the game, shifted the power and introduced real-time influence. The Spread Factor is the additive that drives interaction off the back of content.

My aim here is to deliver an approach that brings together the main elements required to create shareable content. But it will also get you thinking like a media company that exists not just to fill a content schedule but to create potent content that you know your audience wants.

The biggest mistake I see brands make is to focus on social media when they should be focused on *content that creates connection*.

The second biggest mistake big business makes (and here's where entrepreneurs, nimble companies and individuals have an advantage) is that the bigger corporations assign broadcast responsibilities solely to a social media manager or team closely monitored by the PR or marketing department. It's a unit that lives in fear of making a mistake and is closed off from the heart and soul of a business. For social broadcasting to work you need to change team behaviour; you also need to change your behaviour and look outside your designated box for new approaches and ideas. For viral storytelling you need everyone not just involved but fully engaged, understanding what's required and what's at stake.

One thing you can learn from a TV network is that the security guard at the front door is the most important filter in the business. You want this person just as well armed with the ability to pick a good story as your reporters or social media manager. Why? Because stories come in all shapes and sizes from all sorts of sources. If you run a retail store, the customers who visit will deliver you more leads and data around the content you need to be creating than any amount of brainstorming in head office. It's the same in the traditional media ecosystem. The front door of a TV network attracts a colourful cross-section of the community, each with their own story to tell. The person who first greets them needs to know whether or not they are worth the time investment. They are, after all, in the business of storytelling, as you should be too.

You and your staff (if you have any) at all levels need to understand what makes a relevant story for your business. You need to understand what makes an engaging and shareable story for your customers, who are already invested in your brand.

With so many social media gurus scrambling for air time, they have completely overcomplicated the task at hand. The overarching formula is simple:

Content + Distribution = Exposure

That's it. Don't be swayed into believing it's any harder than that.

But as the internet and social media mature and the barriers to entry for creating great content are lowered because phone cameras and software keep getting better, content for content's sake is no longer going to be enough. Quantity versus quality isn't even the equation anymore. The winning formula is an 'Ongoing Quantity of Quality Content'. To compete, it's time to raise your game. Your initial reaction to this news may be overwhelm, that sick feeling in the stomach. 'I'm already busy enough. How can I ever hope to compete?' Don't stress. My experience with helping hundreds of new content creators start their creator/broadcasting journey is that the true root of this discomfort is that they're lost on what content to make and how to make it. The *Like, Comment, Share, Buy* process is about removing that sick feeling, giving you the confidence and guidance you need to find your most effective voice to tell your most contagious stories based not on what you want your business to represent or the brand you wish you were ... but on who you *actually are.*

In achieving this you will have found a position of incredible clarity. All the distractions will evaporate and you will focus all your efforts on achieving the outcomes you seek for yourself and your business. Viral videos, particularly those engineered by brands, always have an outcome in their design. They don't just do it for fun; they are seeking increased levels of engagement, more reach, even lead generation. These are the results that count and the ones you'll enjoy when you create videos with the Spread Factor in their DNA.

Your secret playbook

Understanding the Virable formula, the Spread Factor and how to build on it it will teach you how emotions influence sharing, human psychology, the power of storytelling, how to capture human attention and how to perfect your timing for moments of peak relevance and maximum impact. Think of this formula as your secret playbook for hijacking attention, influencing behaviour and driving real business outcomes through the use of the strategically advanced videos you make yourself.

Viral videos aren't luck, and the term 'viral' shouldn't be scoffed at. They are a force. In fact, they are the pinnacle of successful promotional content, spreading across the internet at a rapid pace at zero distribution cost.

If you believe in social media but aren't looking to create viral content, then you aren't aiming high enough. For one brand viral success might be equated by a million views on YouTube, for another it could be having 80 per cent of their target demographic paying attention to a series of videos.

Whatever your end goal, viral videos should be your target. They represent the highest level of emotional buy-in and trigger the greatest level of interaction. Put simply, viral content spreads the furthest.

How your content is Liked, Commented on and Shared determines its level of exposure, recommendations and consequent sales. No other media platform has made it so easy for you to reach so many for so little. Embrace it. Enjoy it. And look forward to engineering it.

recap:
KEEPING THINGS REAL

- Don't let all the noise around social media overwhelm you. The formula is simple. Content plus distribution equals exposure. These are the only areas to focus on.

- Before you can even think about triggering an action (like Buying) via emotions, you have to (1) capture your viewers' attention and (2) connect with them via a story in order to switch off the thinking brain and turn on the feeling brain.

- The strategy with the lowest risks and greatest returns is to produce an ongoing stream of quality content.

strategy

Listen. Immerse yourself in your audience's world. Be attentive. Be active. And be patient. But most of all, be one of them.

Create groups around the desires or motivations that move your disengaged viewers to be engaged viewers, as identified in the 'Clarifying your context' exercise at the end of chapter 4.

Run polls and livestreams to gain the information you need to remove any doubts around an idea. Your audience will tell you what they want if you give them the chance.

part II: the Virable formula
Unlocking your Viral DNA

So the ground rules are set. Hopefully there has been plenty of thinking, assessment and even some moments of being uncomfortable with how you have been using video thus far on social media. And trust me, that's a good thing.

You have already done the preparation, but now we really start to get to work. The more you challenge what you have always accepted as normal ('That's just the way we have always done things!'), the better. If you are already doing things the right way, then that will become apparent over the next few chapters. I'm not here to change things just for the sake of it. At the same time, I have yet to meet anyone in this space who couldn't benefit from adding another string to their bow.

Before you can start telling your stories, you first need to know where you stand, to understand deeply the role you need to play to trigger the most buy-in from your audience. If you don't know what role you are playing in your own show, your audience, your potential customers, will have no chance of working it out. So the first step is to define your position — to find out who you really are, not just who you want to be.

Once you know where you stand, you need to not only maintain but also defend your position. You have to claim your territory. Right now, social media is a land grab. Every time a new app pops up on the App Store it's a land grab. To defend your space you need to stand strong, to own it. It's all about consistency. And the best way to ensure consistency is to set and follow rules. I'm going to help you craft your own rules around what stories you need to tell and how to tell them.

Your stories, expressed through video, and the commercial benefits they bring to social platforms, are an unbeatable force. This combination drives up both attention rates and 'action' rates — actions like Liking, Commenting, Sharing and Buying. Perhaps the best in the business at this, with a hundred years of experience in developing its time-tested formula, is the Hollywood movie industry. I'll share with you some of their secrets and the moves you can make to have a similar impact on your audience, without the advantage of a Hollywood budget.

You may have doubts about achieving Hollywood-sized responses, but I promise you it all comes down to brain science. You'll discover that many of the secrets used in Hollywood blockbusters are found in viral videos. I'll explain how movie producers hijack attention over and over again, until the audience is primed to respond emotionally and instinctively, and how you can apply the same formulas for your business.

Storytelling is the science you must exploit to market your business in today's world, while preparation and timing are the arts you must master in order to share your stories most effectively. The art of knowing what triggers your audience to stop, engage and spread your message guides all of your timing decisions. I'll walk you through how to gain the knowledge you need in this space that will allow you to plan and strategise a schedule that ensures your video lands at a moment of peak relevance for your audience, at a time when they will most likely want to engage with it.

Through this journey I'll be sharing with you some real examples and case studies for you to watch and dissect for yourselves. You can access all the external resources for the book — the videos and worksheets — via the QR code links that are scattered through the book: simply hold up your phone camera and scan it to gain access.

Before you continue with this book I think it only fair to warn you. What you are about to read will change you. You will never watch videos or movies in quite the same way again.

chapter 6
stay on target

X-Wing pilot 'Gold Five' said it best in *Star Wars: Episode IV — A New Hope*: 'Stay on target.' This is as vital in business as it was for the future of the Rebellion in the movie series. Your ultimate success or failure as a viral video producer will be determined by your ability to remain 'on target' and that's not as easy as it sounds in today's communications environment.

There are many challenges in media and marketing today, but easily the biggest is separating fact from fiction. We have to be on our toes to counter not only the rise of #fakenews but also #fakeinfluencers, #fakerichkids, #fakeentrepreneurs and, my favourite, #fakegetrichquickcoursesonfacebook.

Real, relevant and relatable

The disconnection between what is going on in the world and the world people want us to *believe* they are living in has never been bigger or more confusing. Social media has helped spawn one of the biggest challenges ever in communications — distinguishing between real life and fantasy.

Why is this important? Because successful videos show us that humans still act on instinct. They share the videos they connect deeply to, the videos that are so real, relevant and relatable to their lives that the response to share them is instinctive.

No matter how 'fake' their existence is depicted to be, a user's behaviour remains human. The challenge therefore is on the creators, the communicators, to dig deeper than the Instagram feed of their audience to work out what really makes them tick, not what they want you to believe makes them tick.

To get an idea of where this really began on a mass scale, we need to look back at the birth of popular reality TV. One day this era, which took off in the early 2000s, will be referred to as the 'one small step for content producers' that turned out to be 'one giant leap for content consumers'. Shows like *Survivor* and *Big Brother* drove audiences to believe we were witnessing a massive social experiment played out live in front of our eyes. The first seasons of these types of shows were in fact relatively unscripted and maybe only moderately manipulated. For the most part the contestants played their part the way they saw fit with little to no influence from field producers. As the shows have evolved so too have the fantasy levels and storylines, to the point where they are now often scripted and engineered like any other TV soap. The only difference is that rather than being filmed in makeshift studio sets they use luxurious mansions on exotic tropical islands.

Social media is the *real* reality TV, only the audiences are evolving and responding more rapidly and in more extreme ways. The challenge is how to compete? Social media is littered with tweens through to twentysomethings depicting online lifestyles that rival those of the Kardashians and the Hilton sisters before them. Which is why it's so important that anyone making content understands the true nature of their target market.

There's no shortage of muscled-up lads in fast sports cars on Instagram who, once the phone is put away, are actually still living with their parents, in the bedroom they've occupied since they were five. Or bronzed-up bikini girls who take 15 minutes for the perfect selfie suggesting a life lived in an exotic, luxury location reserved for the rich and famous... at the risk of running late for work at their humdrum, low-paid job. The point is, viral science tells us that 'fake' can gain you attention but almost always at the price of trust. The only time it doesn't work against you is when the audience is in on the joke and the 'sucker' is a common enemy.

The first step to avoiding any hint of fake is understanding who your audience actually is. And I don't mean sitting in a boardroom, developing an avatar of your perfect client and skewing all your communications to this imaginary person, because that in itself is fake. You need to actually invest the time to interact.

Invest time immersing yourself in their culture, listening to how they talk and what they talk about. Observe what and when they post. This is the only way you'll ever work out who your audience really are, what makes them tick, what challenges they face, what changes they want to see. Now, this all sounds like common sense, but you'd be surprised just how many people, brands and corporations fall at this first hurdle. The number one reason they fall at this stage is that they simply take their cues for their content from the pretend world people want us to think they live in. So the creative is based on fake foundations, and that makes it impossible to connect on a real human level.

'Here's a video our audience should like.' I hear this comment, or a close cousin, far too often when a new video is introduced at a marketing department meeting, and it makes me just want to slide under the desk. The audience should like it, right? In a world where we can access more data on our audience than ever before, marketing to them shouldn't be a guessing game. Business shouldn't be a gamble. If you're relying on content to get you customers, then your creative process shouldn't be a digital version of pin the tail on the donkey.

Guessing and hoping is the wrong way to be thinking. Viral videos are always reverse engineered. They work from the audience back to the creative. There's no hoping, no guesswork. There is only a deep understanding of the context and the elements required to trigger a response. Red Bull Media House, for example, ask themselves, 'Is this extreme enough to stimulate our core audience to the point where they will want to share it with other people with similar interests and passions?' From there, all they need to do is put that content in front of those they know won't be able to resist it and the viral cycle will take care of the rest.

So how do you peel away the fake and get to know your real audience? Here are a few simple steps I follow that don't involve hiring expensive research companies. Let me just put it out there: I have a problem with third-party research. Not all of it, not every business that specialises in it, but the investigator in me is very sensitive to 'influence' and leading the respondent, so I like to perform a lot of the observational work myself.

First, I simply listen to their conversations. I don't interact or engage. I just embed myself in the community or group that includes a significant percentage of my potential perfect clients.

After about two weeks of being embedded in the online community, I start to contribute and interact like anyone else. This means leaving any agendas or desires to sell or spruik on silent. This allows me to strategically canvass my audience.

Only once I am in the community will I start to use my presence to collect information. For example, if I am torn over two creative ideas and am not sure which will work best I'll float the ideas in a conversation and see what other people think. I used this tactic to name and position a new product for one of Australia's leading cosmetic brands. The product delivered numerous benefits but I wanted to know which benefit in particular was most potent. The brand's raving fans soon let us know and it has delivered the company a hit niche product that we now know they can't get enough of.

Twitter was once a great place to do this — and don't believe the hype, it still is. You just need to thin out the traffic using some of the search filters to find the information that will prove most valuable when it comes to making the right kind of content for your audience. Look for pop culture references in Twitter handles, around movies and music, or even different kinds of cars or toys. The recent revival of Cabbage Patch Kids is a great example of understanding and targeting a specific niche audience. Kids who had Cabbage Patch Kids in the eighties now have their own children of the right sort of age, so it only makes sense to roll out a 25th anniversary line of the original (or OG) dolls. The sight of Phoebe-Kathleen or Eliza-May is enough to trigger Mum or Dad into a nostalgic journey that drives them to want their own kids to experience what they had ... and of course it all drives sales. This strategy wouldn't have worked at the 10-year or even 15-year anniversary mark. The brains behind the toys understood this. They knew their audience and I have no doubt that social media provided them with the data to get their timing just right.

Even as I write this a video about a toy popular in 1985 called Teddy Ruxpin landed in my feed. My two daughters were fascinated by it. They watched the video then were targeted with a second video, also on Teddy by Kids React on YouTube. They haven't made Teddy Ruxpin story time robot dolls since 2010, but my tip is with 4.6 million views, and if the videos keep popping up as they are, a remake isn't very far away. And here's why.

There's magic and power in what is happening here. At little to no expense the internet is not only conducting the market research for the manufacturers of Teddy Ruxpin, but has taken it a step further.

There's no doubt the videos with millions of views have proved there is a significant level of interest in the toy. But by going viral the already existing popularity has also created further demand. The magic of the internet (if the company had the right strategy in place) is that the manufacturer now has a contact point with their market. With the video now viewed, engaged with and shared, the manufacturer can now re-target those who were stimulated enough by the original video to trigger an action, only the next time round the trigger won't be to share so much as to *buy*. By monitoring the internet, they were able to find, understand and connect with their audience, soon to be customers.

Facebook groups are another way to harness or curate a targeted audience on a specific topic. The best groups for seeding a video are always super niched. When you have a super-niched group it brings a clarity around the triggers that will make the members of the group act and therefore make it easier for you to produce the kind of video that will spread. Remember, it all begins with a handful of people sharing your video with like-minded others, who then will share it on and away you go. If you can't find a group on Facebook that matches your niche, create it, then promote it and nurture those who join it before you try triggering a response. If you start a group and drop a video straight in there you won't gain the traction you are after.

Another way to gain insights into how your audience thinks is via polls. Twitter, Facebook and LinkedIn all have polls, and they are perfect for gathering information and also for letting the majority of your audience drive the creative direction of your brand. Even YouTube, through its cards feature, allows channel managers to run polls against published content.

This opens up a whole new world of learning for creators and brands brave enough to ask questions of their audience about the direction of their content.

Live streams are also starting to emerge as a smart way to better understand your target audience. Live streaming is one of the most authentic ways to connect with your audience. It also allows for personalisation of information to a level never seen before in marketing. Skilled practitioners can respond and redirect a conversation in real time to create viral hype. Live streaming delivers one other element that is breaking down previous barriers.

According to Facebook, interaction and engagement rates on live streams are on average 35 per cent higher than on traditional videos. If you are focused on finding out as much as you can about your audience, this is an interesting stat from a research perspective. Overall though, the Facebook algorithm still appears to put greater weight on the comments on traditional video than those made during live streams. This is believed to be due to the sheer volume of comments on live video.

Get over yourself

Many people I consult with resist giving their audience any influence over the type of content they make. It is as if the content would be less valuable if the idea driving the creative hadn't originated inside their own minds or in head office. To that I say, 'Get out of your own way!' These types of interactions not only benefit you or your brand through the collection of useful data, but your engagement rates will increase dramatically the moment you start serving up the type of content your biggest fans have been waiting for.

If the above scenario puts a twist in your guts, it's time to shift your mindset, make it less about you or your brand and more about the community. It won't take long for you to reap the rewards of increased engagement and loyalty.

Now, while learning and understanding your audience is great, interacting is even better. What you don't want to be doing is rewarding fans with free stuff to gain followers, engagement and increased reach. The Free iPad giveaway strategy I mentioned earlier that infiltrated Facebook is daft. It delivers a short-term spike of interest that does long-term, often irreversible damage to anyone wanting to create shareable, contagious content.

Remember, the viral cycle begins with understanding your real audience and delivering content that triggers increased interactions.

The greater the level of engagement, the further your message will spread. The more contact points you have with your audience, the clearer the picture of them you will be able to build and the more success your videos will enjoy. Knowing the context around how they found you or your brand and why they chose to follow you is vital. If they are there because 12 months ago you gave away a free iPad, then chances are they are waiting for you to give away another one, or they have forgotten about you already and are just too lazy to unfriend you. The point is, if they only followed you for free stuff then there is a good chance they have no real interest in ever buying your products or services. Which means they are even less likely to engage and help spread your content. And by ignoring your videos they are essentially assigning them to an early grave.

If you attract an audience by delivering value, then that is a whole different story.

Your videos should aim to make things easier, to entertain or even to save your viewers time. Your content should be so incredibly relatable that those who view it are triggered to have a conversation that starts along the lines of, 'We were only talking about this the other day...' When you land that response you know you are well tuned in.

The greatest viral video no one ever shared

The other side of content you need to be considering is how does it benefit or reward the people who share or interact with it? About two years into my research I learned this lesson the hard way. Up to this point I had given zero thought to the influence 'self-reflection' would have on the viral outcome of videos. It escaped my thinking and never even registered as an influence when I interviewed a range of experts on human behaviours and psychology. The moment of truth presented itself when I made 'the Greatest Viral Video No One Ever Shared'.

The start of my journey to unlock the secrets of viral videos was actually to start a viral video production company. And what do you think the best way to market a viral video production business is? Of course, make a viral video. I had already enjoyed significant success making videos for some of Australia's top 200 brands and also some emerging start-ups, so it seemed like the perfect time to turn the focus of my hard-won skills to my own business.

The video took months, plenty of dollars and even more favours to produce. I can still clearly remember the night I set the video live to YouTube. I was in my office, in the dark with only the glowing light of my computer screen. My wife and young children were in the room next to my home office watching TV. I had just finished paying the invoices of all the people who helped me make the video and I was down to my last $200. I remember thinking about the strangeness of the position I was in. In one room was my world, everything I live and work for, and with me was a video destined to change it all. To say there was a lot riding on this one video is clearly an understatement. I had spent the day coordinating an army of friends to watch and interact with it to send it viral.

It took about 20 anxious minutes for the first wave of feedback to flow back to me. And when my phone started to 'ping' I've got to be honest with you I really didn't want to look. I was convinced my friends would think it sucked.

They didn't. The feedback was overwhelming. 'This is awesome.' 'Incredible job.' 'What a crazy-ass video!'

This was the start of my problems. I was so caught up in the emotions of the moment, in the relief of receiving positive feedback, that I hadn't noticed one glaring issue, the one problem that would consign this video to the murky depths of YouTube's 'less than 1000 views' category.

To this day it is still one of the best cinematic pieces of video I've ever made, but as a viral video to launch a viral video business it bombed, sucked, wiped out. I was wanting way more than 1000 views; in fact, less than a thousand was probably more damaging than no video at all in this scenario.

What I had failed to notice was that all that glowing feedback wasn't happening in the comments section of the video. The comments were coming via text messages and therefore not contributing to firing the algorithm that was responsible for sending stuff viral.

I could get friends to watch it, but I couldn't get them to engage. I had misread my audience. I had made the video I wanted to make because I thought it was cool and it sat well on the feeds of my social profiles. But the audience or customer journey was all wrong. I was missing a bridge, so no one was completing the total engagement process required.

It was this. I am a Creative and I am also my own boss and my own HR department, so I rarely encounter any issues with the things I choose to post online. But most of my network aren't in this category, and 'the Greatest Viral Video No One Ever Shared' was too heavy and risky for them to engage with. They knew if they did it would appear on their newsfeeds, and it worried them.

I had given no consideration to how this video would reflect on those who shared it.

I don't take losses, only lessons, and this is one of the most important lessons I learned while researching viral content.

What people post and share is always a reflection of themselves, even the fake wannabe version. If a piece of content conflicts with that self-image, you have zero chance of getting them to engage with it — to take the Like, Comment, Share, Buy journey that drives business.

Viral videos get it right, breaking out of the pack, when they benefit or reward the people who help distribute their content. I'm not talking about gifts or cash prizes. Today the right content, with the right messaging that sparks the right conversations is worth way more than money. If your content can enhance the standing of the person sharing it, particularly their standing among their peers, then you'll have a loyal follower for ever.

For example, you already know I'm a massive *Star Wars* fan. As the *Star Wars* guy within my social networks I'm always the first to share the best news and content on the topic. The better the content, the stronger my standing and identity as the go-to authority among my friends. Join my social circle and start posting *Star Wars* content and you'll be in more trouble than Han Solo in carbonite ... lol.

Equally, viral videos enhance the standing of the viewer among a peer group that appreciate the same types of video. And you can't just trip over that kind of influence — it comes from a deep understanding of what makes your target audience tick.

Let's just unpack that last point a little further. I've already said this but I believe it so strongly I feel the need to reinforce it. In this current environment, content is currency and great content in the current sea of noise is hard to find. As smart as the algorithms are, as good as the creators are at targeting, there is no better recommendation than one from the people you love and trust. Those people have already taken the risk to watch a video for you. And by sharing it with others they are giving it their stamp of approval. In your mind you already know it has passed a certain standard, risk is removed and now there's even a component of FOMO at play. All these things drive the viral cycle, but none of them happen if you don't first understand who you are communicating with.

It is little about the content you want to make and everything about the content they want to consume. Keep that in mind the next time you are thrashing out some video ideas and land on one that your target audience 'should' like.

recap:
AIM HIGHER AT THE START
OF YOUR VIEWER FUNNEL

- Being relevant leads to engagement, growth and some $$ being ...

    Hyper-relevant => more engagement => more growth => more $$

- So you need to push your boundaries.

- Establish your unique position.

- Understand that connection with an audience is delicate. Any inconsistency will increase the chances that they'll simply move on.

exercise:
ESTABLISHING BRAND
STORY CLARITY

In the exercise at the end of chapter 4, I asked you to define your brand by answering a simple question, 'Who are you?', in 25 words or less. Now let's review that brand statement and measure it for clarity.

Simply answer these questions about your description.

Would someone reading it understand not only   YES/NO
what you do but why you do it?

Does it inspire them to act?   YES/NO

Could they explain what you do to someone else?   YES/NO

And when they do, are they using your words?   YES/NO

Is it clear who you are talking to?   YES/NO

If you answered NO to any of these questions, then sorry, the foundations of your brand story aren't clear enough. Identify the gap(s) in your initial brand statement and rewrite it until you return at least 4 out of 5 YES answers.

chapter 7
brand story clarity ▶

Only with a complete understanding of the nuances of your audience can you take the first step of the Virable formula. I call this step Brand Story Clarity, because every engineered viral video is produced by a brand that possesses complete clarity around who they are.

If your videos are failing to find traction, cut-through or engagement, it will often be here that you'll discover your greatest opportunities for improvement. Don't be afraid to revisit this step if things aren't working out right for you.

There's no point in producing any content if you don't know what you want your customer to believe in.

Once you are crystal clear on your Brand Story, whatever you create after that will have a 'print', a 'sense' of what your brand legacy is about, an 'invisible impact' that acts like an identifier — it's like the difference between a friend at your front door and a stranger.

A strong motivator for sharing is the conviction in the value and benefit of that video. Sometimes it will feel almost like a crime, or at least a missed opportunity, not to share it and move ahead of the pack.

The Virable formula works like market research, a taste-testing score card. It delivers a score out of 100 based on the viewer's inputs into our algorithm. A video may score 75 out of 100 but to spread, to attract the engagement it needs to fire, we know it needs to score 80. It can be just a subtle difference that makes all the difference; whether or not an action is triggered may rest on no more than 5 to 10 points on the scale.

The difference could relate to a minor element that is nonetheless hyper-relevant to your audience at the time — anything from an ongoing in-joke to being really clear about how this video fits into your overall brand story. When you weigh up the outcomes, these 'small' differences aren't small at all, and it all starts with a clear understanding of your brand story and finding those invisible connections that deliver the added impact.

(Just one way YouTubers convey these connections is by displaying familiar items in the background of their camera shots: memorabilia of particular significance to the key demographic's tribe, cultural references that, by providing recognisable links, draw people together.)

Clarity around your identity, narrative and purpose adds important elements to the framework: it establishes your starting point, cements your position and identifies what you need to be for your audience. Only if you are true to your purpose can you continue to work on creating more content.

I've seen great creators strike it rich in views but be left feeling hollow and empty because they compromised their purpose to achieve internet fame. Sure, it was a high at the time, but eventually they are left despondent and confused about the path to take moving forward. Do they continue to compromise their beliefs to chase cheap fame or do they work to rediscover their sense of purpose? Often they opt to make no decision at all and so end up making no more content.

Position

Let's begin by looking at position.

Well beyond having a side or an opinion, your position dictates who you are and how you communicate your message. This influences the way you speak, the story you tell, the style of video you make and the issues you choose to make the video about. Once you are clear, all of these elements provide your audience with a context they find relevant. This in turn drives engagement and ultimately grows your business.

Adding a Viral DNA to this formula, the process we are working on and refining in this book, increases the overall impact exponentially.

> **hyper-relevant => more engagement =>**
> **more growth => more \$\$**

The power of brand story clarity is that it forces you to form a set of values that lead to your delivery of a consistent message.

Brands that have a clear story never waver from who they are; they have a deeper understanding of what their customer believes in and what they must stand for to maintain not only their customer's trust but also their attention.

Back in the 1980s, when they were fighting for market share: Apple made a strategic decision that still dictates the identity of their business today: rather than chasing the saturated sports market or big business, Apple chose the 'crazy ones' — the creatives, the dreamers, the different thinkers.

Their brand story is clear and evident in all their decisions — from product to marketing and through to retail experience. Unique. 'So Apple.' Set on 'Thinking Different', and standing by it, they aren't distracted or swayed by trends and temptations. There's a consistent familiarity about any experience you have with them as a company.

The result is that a large part of the population that are fighting to be recognised as creative, unique and different are drawn to the ideals manifested by Apple. And because Apple has given them a 'place', whenever they drop a video there is an audience hungry not only to consume it but to share it with other unique and different individuals.

Like a tsunami, all viral videos start with a small wave. You need to find your unique position. Every individual has a different story, as every business has a unique proposition and every news story has different potential angles.

I find it fascinating, for example, that when news reporters, who are often trained at the same universities and have a similar social background, are sent to cover the same story or event, they can come up with a quite different take on it, and that each of these will resonate with a different audience. It's how we are. People are different; they'll often make different assessments and draw different conclusions.

It's much the same with your videos. Each one will have an audience, but it never works to try to make a video for everyone. The connection with the audience is fragile; any inconsistency in who you are and what you stand for will break that link.

You need a lot of things to go right to create a viral video, and this is the first.

The heightened benefits are revealed when you start applying brand story clarity to the mechanics of social platforms. Online, like-minded people hang out together, partly because the internet gods group us together so it's easier for marketers to hit us up. The potential advantage for content creators, entrepreneurs and brands is in understanding all the nuances when launching a viral cycle.

I've already spoken about the benefit of targeting a key demographic and triggering them to share with their friends and others of like mind, who are likely to respond to the same triggers. Psychologists call this creating a 'positive viral co-efficient'. As long as the co-efficient has a positive value greater than 1 it will continue to be shared, creating a viral spread. The higher the co-efficient the faster the spread. Equally, the larger the seed audience the faster the spread.

On the flip side, if you post or create content that doesn't have clarity or isn't aligned with your brand, even as an individual, you will lose your audience. Chances are you'll confuse them and they'll no longer trust you. This happens a lot to thought leaders who spend Monday to Friday posting about their area of expertise, but lose momentum on the weekends when they share random videos about their everyday life. In the worst case, your audience will move on, or they will stay but won't be prepared to put their names to any actions.

So let me share a story about a client of mine whom I was lucky enough to have worked with for a few years. This brand, a performance sports brand, came to market as a disruptive company in the most competitive clothing market on the planet, sports apparel. They are taking on Nike, Adidas, Reebok — all the big guys.

Right from the beginning this company had a really clear brand story, which helped them grow at an incredible rate. Everything was expertly aligned. In their case they were positioned in the market as a get the best out of your performance 'badass'. This is reflected in their name, the clothing they produce, the athletes they sponsor, the imagery they use and the content they produce ... most of the time.

The result was that they were able to rapidly attract an army of hard-core believers. Consistency gave them traction in a crowded market.

This goes well beyond branding, cool logos and colours. You can have an awesome-looking brand but if what you are communicating doesn't reach out and connect, if your videos are lame, you are going to lose.

If you are an individual or a small business, you replace 'sponsor' with who you publicly associate with, the podcasts you make guest appearances on, the websites you seek PR from, the collaborations you do. All these elements build *your unique Viral DNA*.

The sports apparel company focused on performance and ensuring those who wear their clothes get the most out of life. They vowed never to make garments that didn't deliver a performance benefit. Run faster, swim stronger, ride longer, train better, recover quicker. The content they were posting always focused, not on the products, but on improving performance — training tips, science and advantages. The brand story being told by the company was pretty clear. We are about helping you perform at your peak.

The best way of illustrating how powerful brand story clarity can be is by giving an example of when a brand happens to get it wrong.

The same sports apparel company had been through a period of significant growth, scaling from 10 to 100 staff in less than a year. In that period of rapid growth it's fair to say their social media presence wasn't a big priority. The growth in audience was solid but the overall numbers weren't on a par with the bigger players in their space, who had a massive head start when it came to brand loyalty and mass market storytelling.

There came a time when the social media growth of this brand started to stagnate. Engagement became sporadic then started to slump. This negatively affected online traffic numbers and eventually sales.

What was causing the disconnection? Maybe the social platforms had changed their algorithm? Maybe their competitors were targeting their customers with better offers? Or maybe, just maybe, the content they were posting was no longer aligned to their brand story.

So what caused their sales to slow down? You'd never guess... not in a million guesses.

Bircher muesli.

Yep. Photos and recipes focused on healthy eating. It was definitely one of those 'our followers should like this content' scenarios.

Here's what happened. With the big investor buy-in coming they had turned the screws a little to get the most out of every aspect of the business. The social media team studied the brands with bigger followings to see how they might improve their results. They saw that those accounts regularly posted images of healthy meals, sunsets and yoga all over Instagram. It was evidently working for these brands; it only made sense it could work for them too, so they added similar posts to their marketing mix.

For three weeks they religiously inserted food and lifestyle posts into their content schedule. They didn't abandon their core offering of performance-based information and inspiration; they just added the lifestyle angle.

Can anyone see the problem here? Surely it was a move to reach more people, a new audience they hadn't previously attracted. But Bircher muesli didn't have a place within the performance-based story of this brand. By adding the lifestyle posts they'd confused their audience by being inconsistent. They'd stepped outside their channel boundaries and as a result had derailed their entire online brand story. What they stood for, what their products did — nothing was clear anymore.

It left the audience questioning whether they still believed in them or wanted to be part of the tribe. They were no longer sure if they identified with the brand. Lifestyle didn't represent the values they were originally attracted to.

For some, losing the clarity meant also losing the trust, and this reflected on them, so they no longer wanted to interact. And if the audience wasn't interacting, they weren't taking action, which meant the content wasn't spreading and the audience wasn't moving closer to the buying decision moment that drives sales.

So how do you fix it? It isn't as easy as just switching back to the old ways. You have to realign the channel and reinstate the clarity in your story.

Picture it. You have a channel with boundaries. Every video you make needs to sit in this bowling alley runway in order to knock over the viewers waiting patiently at the end of the lane.

But Bircher muesli…? That lane is way over on the other side of the room. So to fix the disruption, to save and reinforce the connection with the audience—because the damage is done; it's taken a hit—you have to counterbalance it. Like a piece of elastic, you have to overstretch things past the original position for a short time for it to settle back to where you really need it to sit. You need to bowl a few strikes down a lane a couple over.

For the brand in question, they handled the next stage really well by taking things to another level. They turned to a group for whom a sub-par performance can mean the difference between life and death—the US Navy Seals. More than most, these guys clearly need a performance advantage.

And it worked. A broadcast line-up of video content hosted by former Navy Seals, military-grade exercise physiologists and medical practitioners won back the trust of the hardcore performance athletes. The value and insights communicated were at a level way beyond the experience of the audience, which boosted their interest and engagement. Within weeks you had to scroll a long way back to find any trace of the lifestyle-inspired posts as the core brand story began to be reinstated. Social posts focused on performance, reflecting the products built only for performance. Followers started to trust them again and as a result sales bounced back, increasing by 33 per cent over the following three months.

The lesson in this when it comes to making videos, or any type of content, can be summed up in *the Three C's of content creation*:

1. clarity

2. connection

3. conversion.

You could have everything right — product, store location, price … everything — but if your communications, your videos, are off even slightly, it can cost you. On the flip side — because I'm a glass-half-full kinda guy — get it right and the customers you've been so desperately looking for will be just there waiting for you to show up.

To achieve brand story clarity, you *must* stand for something that makes it very clear who you are. Who you are must be so ingrained in everything you do that it's like a company religion, the purpose that drives you, your reason for being, beyond 'making money'. Many brands and businesses already do this internally but they fail to communicate it successfully in the current media environment.

Beliefs

Clarity and purpose are the oxygen you need to deliver a successful video-driven campaign. Because the audience now invites you into their world, they demand to know you better. They want to know that your purpose aligns with their personal beliefs. And as long as you continue to satisfy their beliefs they won't go looking for satisfaction elsewhere.

Viral brands understand this deeply. They radiate extreme clarity around the way they communicate and the format in which they do so. This comes from fully understanding your audience's needs and wants.

Social media is a place for humans, and your business or brand is judged on a human level on its overall personality and behaviours. Individuals, brands and businesses that market on social platforms are discovering they have to 'humanise' their messaging in order to interact successfully. This is a massive shift from traditional marketing.

One of the biggest challenges you will struggle with as a creator is keeping your great ideas aligned with your brand story. It's a challenge I face every day. I can come back home from a walk or run with the greatest idea for a video, only to remind myself to stop and consider, 'Is this great creative idea also great for my business?'

It's important to remember that what triggers one brand's video to go viral won't work for another. From your position of brand story clarity, parameters emerge. Picture your channel as a dead straight road on a desert highway. Every time you leave your lane, you crash into something. Soon your car is covered in dints, not looking nearly as shiny and attractive as it would have if you'd just stayed in your lane.

You may meet new people, and people may learn you, but they're not heading in the same direction, not tuned in to your channel. They don't need you and they aren't going to help spread your message; ultimately they would never buy from you. Your audience will come for the journey only if they know they can trust you aren't going to change course, that you aren't going to change lanes and take them somewhere they don't want to go.

I call it the hitchhiker principle. You are trying to hitch a ride and a truck pulls up and asks where you're heading. You reply, 'Just to the next town.'

If the truck driver says, 'Okay, I'm heading straight there', you feel confident you're about to be taken where you want to go.

But what if the truck driver says, 'Oh, okay, I can take you there, but first I need to drop some things off down the end of that dirt road before making a quick detour to a small town on the other side of those hills, then I can swing by the town you're heading for.' The promise is still there, but you aren't feeling nearly so confident.

Now, you may be thinking what has this got to do with videos?

The answer is 'everything', if you want them to drive engagement and build a following. If you want those Likes, Comments and Shares, and the Buy-in, you need to be clear about what path you are on and what the audience is going to get in return if they continue on this journey with you.

What we are digging down into is true authenticity — being who you say you are, delivering the lessons that your brand story promises to deliver.

It's a while ago now but let's go back to 2014 for a great example of a brand failing to deliver on its promise. Pepsi produced a video to welcome in the New Year. It involved setting up 2014 mousetraps in a room and dropping 2015 ping pong balls on top of them. (During the COVID-19 pandemic of 2020 a similar video was made to show how the virus can be community transmitted if people don't take the proper precautions.)

Pepsi's idea is primed for the internet: it's crazy enough to be shared; the number of traps and balls made it relevant for the new year date; and the visual impact is not only astonishing but highly relatable, because viewers can see themselves being able to perform a similar stunt at home or in their university dorm.

But here's the thing. For marketing eternity Pepsi has been fighting off the charge that they are nothing but Coca-Cola's little brother, that they are the imitator in the Cola wars. Up until that point all their online content was linked to musicians and rappers, being unique, different and cool. This video was one of their first attempts at being socially savvy online, to create shareable content.

Scan QR code
to watch the
video

And they were sure they were onto a winner. After all, the concept had already gone viral because a university science department had pulled it off four years earlier...

Wait ... What?

That's right. Pepsi had lifted the idea from a video made by a university science department that had already gone viral and tried to make it their own.

Now this video was being shared by Pepsi lovers ... right up to the point (about three days later) when they discovered it was a rip-off, the point when Coca-Cola and a conga-line of social media commentators took wicked delight in calling Pepsi out. Those that Liked, Commented and Shared the video were embarrassed when 'friends' in their social circles pointed out the con. Pepsi left their fans feeling duped, as though they had been tricked. Former enthusiastic fans were left wondering whether interacting with Pepsi content was worth the risk. In a cruelly ironic twist, the little brother in the Cola wars tried to pull off a stunt that ultimately evoked the behaviour of a little brother trying to punch above his weight. Sadly for them, they got caught.

Understand that brand story clarity stops you from looking to others for ideas. It stops you from making the same mistake that Pepsi made. Because more often than not the ideas that work for others won't work for you.

So now you have an understanding of why brand story clarity is vitally important when it comes to video marketing, how do you develop it? What are the steps you need to take?

Marketers have used many methods over the years to develop strong, clear brands but there is one that works particularly well with storytelling, especially when you are trying to embed human traits into content built for a brand.

As I studied those 1200 viral videos, I began to see a pattern forming around the assumed knowledge viewers had of the videos — that is, the stories they were sharing, the lessons they were teaching, even the personalities of the creators behind the content.

International brand expert Simon Hammond, the founder of Be Brands and author of the bestselling book of the same name, introduced me to how he establishes unique brand positions based on beliefs.

Hammond builds and rescues iconic brands by developing a religious beliefs system around what a brand stands for — their purpose beyond the product. The videos I was dissecting in order to uncover the secret to viral triggers were all success stories in terms of their spread across the internet. All viral, they all appeared to have strong correlations with purpose-driven brands. It became obvious at an early stage that there is a link between having a purpose that people want to be part of and the ability to consistently create viral videos they want to support by Liking, Commenting and Sharing.

Before you push the red record button, you first need a deep understanding of your audience. You should already be thinking about your purpose in this space and how to communicate it to gain traction and viewer action.

The art of viral videos is based not only on how clearly you understand the data you have collected but on how clearly you translate that data in the next step.

More than simply forming a mission statement, Hammond encourages brands to develop beliefs. What is the brand there to do? What does it stand for? What is its overarching purpose? I have tweaked Hammond's method to fit more naturally with a storytelling/video marketing approach, but the following exercise should help you work towards greater brand story clarity.

Complete this exercise to help develop greater clarity around your story and the role you play in your ideal customer's life. Remember, there is no point telling stories online unless you are certain of the role you are playing in the production.

recap:
IN VIDEO WE TRUST

- Capture and develop your brand values into a 'religion'. It will make them more readily understood and easier for others to 'buy' into.

- Who you are is communicated in more ways than just the videos you produce, and it must all be aligned, from your brand name, the level at which you speak, the platforms you use and the people/brands you collaborate or interact with.

exercise:
BUILDING A BRAND STORY
PEOPLE BELIEVE IN

At the end of chapter 6 you worked on bringing real clarity to the foundations of your brand story. Now we need to focus on that statement a little more in order to extract your brand beliefs from it, the non-negotiables that will set you apart from everyone else.

First, for greater clarity (especially if you're a visual learner like me), imagine a conversation between two people in which it would be natural for you, your brand or your business to be brought up.

Now, take note of the picture you just painted in your head, because it will hold clues.

- Who are the two people?

- How do they know each other?

- What are their general conversation topics?

- Where is the conversation taking place?

Don't be afraid to get really specific about the scene you are drawing in your mind's eye. (Trust me, the type of sugar on the table of a café can speak volumes about the customers that visit and the things they tend to believe in. Is it that mud sugar the hipsters go for or is it white, refined kid sugar?) By working through this scenario, you should be becoming really clear on who your key audience is and what triggers them.

You need to understand these people deeply, including:

- the challenges they face in life

- what scares them

- what they desire

- what stops them from achieving their goals (not their excuses, but what really stops them).

It is these responses that will form the platform for your belief statement and content mantra. For example, this is the brand belief, mantra and tag for my company Virable. I think you will find that it makes it very clear what we do and why we do it.

Virable

Mantra: Viable Viral Videos

Tag: It takes someone who's been there to take you there.

Belief: Why seek to go viral and then seek to play it safe?

My whole life has been about media impact as an art form while ensuring the train never runs out of control.

It's about maximum impact without damage to you, your brand or your customers.

My objective is to create viral heroes whose reputations skyrocket.

My personal version of these statements sits in my purpose which I introduced to you right at the start of the book.

I am out to save the internet ... one bad video at a time.

Individuals and brands that repeatedly create viral videos have all laid (almost fortified) brand beliefs as their foundations. And viewers of their content, even if they aren't raving fans, already have some assumed knowledge about the characteristics of the content they are about to watch. The process you have just followed is designed to help you form your own brand story foundations.

Start by writing out your belief statement. Four of five lines that address the challenges your customers face, what scares them, what they desire and what is stopping them from achieving those goals.

_____

_____

_____

_____

_____

Next, extract your tag line from your belief. This is a short statement that sums up your overall advantage and speaks directly to the fears of your ideal customer.

And finally, your mantra. This is a short, succinct statement or arrangement of words that states what you do.

chapter 8
rules of engagement ▶

Trust is built on clarity and consistency. Once you have established clarity around your brand, the next step is to maintain it consistently. To do so without any guides is beyond an art; it's downright risky. Remember the hitchhiker or, if you prefer, the bowling alley metaphor, in the previous chapter? This chapter is devoted to some strategies for staying on track, in your own lane, even when the biggest creative ideas you've ever dreamt up pop into your head.

One of the biggest misconceptions around social media and audiences is that only brands with polished, big-budget content attract big followings. It simply isn't true. People choose to follow brands or include them in their feeds for a number of different reasons. Engaging content is just one. Now, producing outstanding social media content is never a bad idea; even great content will do nicely. But because it is an expression or extension of your business and also a place to engage and interact, there is a risk you could lose followers or damage your brand if you appear out of reach or even too polished and therefore expensive. You need to ensure you get the balance right.

When you play in the social media space, it's always a good idea to minimise risk. The key to success is to build on a steady effort you've put in over time rather than inconsistently, erratically, through a presence that spikes but never grows.

Content that operates creatively within the recognised boundaries of what makes your brand clear ensures that you constantly deliver to your audience the types of videos that ensure the greatest level of engagement, because increased engagement always leads to growth.

Frames of reference

An early episode of *The Simpsons* tells the biblical narrative of Moses and the Ten Commandments, and every time I catch it on repeat I wonder if this is where I drew inspiration for developing this step of the system. The Ten Commandments were essentially rules for living righteously. They gave the people behavioural boundaries — lanes within which to operate safely, if you like.

Most of the world's great commercial brands have mottos, catchphrases or mantras, like the ones you worked on in the previous chapter. You'll find them proudly displayed on the walls in the reception area at head office or in the header of their websites. These statements define the principles and philosophy of the business, what's expected from staff, the culture they nurture for success. As a staff member, either you buy into these principles or you go find another job.

They are a frame of reference to guide your decision making and shape how your busines is conducted. If they don't feel like a good fit you should jump ship, because you can only fake it for so long and it's never going to end well.

In a broadcast model there is a need for a similar frame of reference. On an operational level it ensures the consistent storytelling your audience seeks. It provides clarity, a transparent starting point from which you can confidently create, discuss and refine your ideas.

I call this frame of reference your 'rules of engagement' (ROE).

Defining your ROE, much like your belief system, can be a brutal process. It should draw on the input of a wide range of informed opinions — whether that's key stakeholders for a brand or business, or mentors and your inner circle for individual creators building a personal brand.

When defining your rules of engagement, don't make them complicated or too numerous. Three to five of them work best. Their role is as a consistent guide to ensure your creative ideas and actions are always aligned with your brand voice.

TV stations have been using rules to manage their creative output for decades. With entrepreneurs and brands emerging as the broadcasters of the new era, it's clear that the best of them have learned a thing or two from the giants that went before them.

A simple way to look at how ROEs influence the creative output of content is to study how TV stations cover daily news. On a number of Australia's commercial networks, news bulletins are scattered throughout the daily broadcast schedule — from early-morning breakfast news programs, to midday news bulletins, afternoon news, prime-time news, public affairs news and sometimes even late-night news.

Despite all these programs being broadcast on the same station, and in recent times relying on a lot of the same staff, the way they cover the same events can be very, very different. Breakfast shows are traditionally more light-hearted and conversational. Afternoon news is more conventional but will often feature guests and casual discussions. The prime-time bulletin is serious and hard-hitting rather than seeking to entertain. Public affairs news programs look to gain as many viewers as possible through a tabloid style of storytelling.

Rules determine what types of stories best fit which programs, and when a story is big enough to be mentioned in all bulletins across the day, the style in which that story is told will vary markedly.

The respective programs have their own creative boundaries to best serve the audience at the time of going to air. Over the past five decades, TV networks have come to learn and refine what it is the audience of each show wants and how they want it packaged.

Benefits of ROEs

You have to determine your own creative boundaries, your own rules of engagement to capture the attention of your audience with the least resistance. On social media, instead of having different personas for different times of the day, you need them for each individual platform. Remember, 'Do you', but how you package your story or message must meet the expectations of the audience on the given platform.

The greatest benefit of setting ROEs is consistency. Whether you make the videos yourself or contract a third party such as an agency or production company or, as you scale up, bring in a social media/content manager, as long as the producer understands and abides by the rules, you can't go wrong. You can even use them to run consumer-generated content campaigns, increasing the likelihood that the videos you receive from your followers are also on brand.

Red Bull is a brand that has real clarity in its story and rules around the videos it produces. Mention the name and most people can instantly picture a Red Bull-style video. It's as though the product they're trying to sell you, the can of energy drink, is secondary. And the truth is, it is.

Dove is another brand that seems to be able to drop viral videos whenever it wants. Since the hugely successful Sketches campaign, Dove has wielded real power in the social ecosystem. Their rules around social video, which focus heavily on empowering women to value themselves, have produced many a massive winner for them.

tip

Where do your rules come from? They are drawn directly from your mantra and brand positioning. They need to filter out ideas, even great ideas, that don't represent the voice your customers connect with. And they should allow anyone from within your inner circle or business to understand if an idea is worthy or not of being posted.

If your communications can't be understood by a 12-year-old, then in this fast-paced world people will tune out and move on. This applies as much to your customers as to your staff. So find clarity and keep it simple:

To help to define your rules, begin by asking these questions:

- What do you do that others don't?

- Where are you that others aren't?

- Why did your audience follow you rather than your competition?

Rules of engagement have another incidental yet significant upside. Rather than depending on one or two team members to come up with all your creative ideas, ROEs allow everyone in your business to pitch concepts without fear of rejection. They give people confidence that their ideas have value, and you end up with more ideas than ever. You will never struggle to fill a content schedule again.

As an illustration, here are the ROEs for my company, Virable:

1. Move it or lose it. Moving pictures move people.

2. Real, relevant and relatable.

3. Kick me, hit me, but just don't sh!t me.

4. We hate ads. People buy, you can't sell.

5. There is no TRY — only TRY-BAL.

What kind of picture do these rules paint of my business and the way we work? And when we apply these rules to the videos we produce to promote ourselves, what boundaries have been set?

Here's a more literal summary of the rules that essentially define our values and in turn attract the right kinds of audiences to improve our engagement and conversions.

1. We only play with video, because video is dominant.

2. The nature of our content can't be fake.

3. Push the boundaries but be conscious of not being annoying.

4. We don't make ads, because we know the wider internet community works hard to avoid them.

5. Understand and operate within the beliefs of the community.

Now it's time for you to formulate your own rules — just three to five straightforward, non-negotiable ROEs. If you are a 'discount' car wash, then the rules that define your content need to reflect that you offer the best price in town, and that better be true. If you are a 'prestige' car wash, you need to be charging premium prices and you better live up to the premium claim.

See how you go setting your rules.

recap:
NOT ALL RULES ARE MEANT TO BE BROKEN

- Consistency is key.

- Create only three to five simple rules that envelop your values — simple enough that you should be able to write them on your wall.

- Don't be lured or romanced by what others are doing. Do you.

- Rules of engagement allow everyone in your business to pitch concepts without fear of rejection.

exercise:
ESTABLISHING YOUR RULES
OF ENGAGEMENT

From your belief statement and with your brand personality in mind, extract three to five points, statements or positions that make you or your brand unique.

Answering the following questions will trigger the types of advantages you are trying to isolate:

What's the/your ambition?

_____

What's the risk?

_____

What's the plan?

_____

Why are you different?

_____

What do you stand for?

_____

These need to be the things you know through experience and knowledge in your industry vertical. And they need to be non-negotiable.

While isolating your three to five non-negotiables, think about building a fortress around your unique brand position, constants that won't waver anytime soon.

_____

_____

_____

_____

_____

Now let's go back and really cross-examine what you have come up with. The more scrutiny you apply here, the stronger your rules will be.

Do any of the points you listed above affect each other? Do they double up? (Typically, candidates who do this exercise in my course end up with points that deliver the same outcome — they just express it in a different way. So watch out for that.)

Are there any points that contradict each other?

Let's take these points and craft them into your ROE.

_____

_____

_____

_____

_____

_____

_____

_____

chapter 9
the art and science of storytelling

▶

To this point we have been identifying your audience and establishing the strategies to maintain a consistent brand narrative in your videos, the steps required to engage a viewer and potential future customer. The next steps focus on how to hold that viewer's attention, blocking out all distractions, for long enough to stimulate them to take action.

These are the foundations for successful video making, because this is where the connections are made both with the viewer's brain and with the algorithm measuring the interaction. It is much easier to capture the audience's attention when your videos are relevant, focusing on topics of current interest that touch on their lives.

If you have delivered relevant content to a viewer previously, then it is easier to attract their attention again as their resistance is lowered. As the trust builds up, this viewer will become part of your regular audience. Keep delivering and you'll soon have the chance to convince them to take action — buying your products or services, perhaps.

Stopping people scrolling through their newsfeed is a challenge. Having them watch is an investment. Triggering them to buy is both an art and a science.

Here's the most common sequence. A viewer has watched your video, which has piqued their interest. They are persuaded by what you or your business stands for. Perhaps they identify with you. In any case, there is the potential for you to deliver a return on their investment of the time it takes to watch. This assessment cycle continues in a viewer's mind until they become fully engaged with what you are offering or they break off the engagement. Just like a fish teasing a fisherman's bait, you've caused their thumb to stop scrolling... it's a nibble. You still need to get them on the hook and there is still plenty of work to do to land them in your boat.

Contrary to some commentary comparing our supposed falling attention span with that of a goldfish, it's not the human brain that is changing — it's the quality of the content. On the internet, you have a window of approximately 8 to 20 seconds, depending on the platform, to convince your audience to keep watching your content. So you either need to learn to speak really fast or learn the powerful, time-tested art of storytelling. Because, as I'll explain a little later, only storytelling has the power to buy you more time with the viewer.

Storytelling is a hot topic right now. You only have to spend a few minutes on LinkedIn to notice that 'Storyteller' as an occupation is growing at least as fast as 'Entrepreneur'.

A good working definition of 'story' (from dictionary.com) is 'a narrative, either true or fictitious, in prose or verse, designed to interest, amuse, or instruct the hearer or reader; tale'. In a practical sense, a story is a sequence of related events retold and linked in a way that is not only receptive to the brain, but readily understood. I think there couldn't be a more useful thing for marketers and business owners, let alone internet or social media marketers, to learn and remember.

If I learned anything from my five years of research into videos and my time in advertising and journalism it is that people tend to overcomplicate their message. Whether that's by being too 'clever' or too 'edgy', the outcome is the same: the work fails to be understood.

Social media marketing is overwhelmingly overcomplicated. Ads, SEO, content, algorithms, watch times, session starts, multiple platforms, thumbnails... the list goes on.

While I accept that understanding and implementing at least some of the above may help you, the more I pull apart great viral campaigns, the more I help others reverse their fortunes with video, the more it reinforces for me that there are two elements you should be fully focused on before looking anywhere else. These are:

1. ensuring your content is receptive to the brain

2. making certain it is easily understood.

The core components of great content. Without them your videos are guaranteed to fail. Yet despite their significance, they are by far the most under-researched and under-invested areas in marketing.

I want to change that. Right here. Right now, with you.

The brain is designed to receive and recall information in a particular pattern or sequence. The better you are at delivering your information the way the brain wants to receive it, the less resistance you will experience in the initial engagement phase and the lower the chances of you losing their attention because of an outside distraction.

In a noisy environment like social media, that offers you a massive advantage.

The second element is comprehension. How readily is your message understood? At school, you may remember teachers conducting running records on your reading abilities and asking you questions afterwards. They were measuring whether you were just reading the words or actually understanding them.

To trigger the viral sequence, your viewer must not only 'watch' your message but firmly grasp its meaning. Comprehension is key for carrying a viewer, reader or listener from automatically processing words to actually developing emotional responses to a situation or scenario inside a story. I'll explain this in more detail in the following chapter, but essentially, to get them to share, you first need to get them to care. There's a bridge you need your customers to cross before they'll even consider Liking, Commenting, Sharing or Buying.

That bridge is story.

Stories capture and hold attention

Because the human brain is largely instinctive and hasn't evolved nearly as fast as technology, there are two ways to measure if your videos lack all the elements required to be classified as 'storytelling': first, if you are posting videos and your average watch time or retention is low and your viewers are bailing within seconds; second, if people have watched your video but they struggle to recall what it was about.

Retaining the attention of the viewer and memory recall are the greatest benefits of true storytelling; both play a key role in the success of online content in all its forms.

Stories have the power to hijack a viewer's brain and hold their attention for longer, increasing watch time and buying you more time to form a connection and trigger feelings in the viewer. Stories also increase the rate of recall or memory because they deliver information in a way the brain likes to file it away.

First, let's focus on *attention*.

Science tells us that the human brain is the most selfish organ in the human body. As an extreme illustration, if you are drowning, the brain will steal oxygen from your other organs to make sure it lives the longest — or, if you prefer, dies last.

It's also important to recognise that the human brain has a lot going on. For starters, it is keeping us alive, monitoring our environment, making decisions, evaluating decisions, calculating energy levels and looking out for threats. In modern society, even without the danger of sabre-toothed tigers to worry about, it is still quite a workload, so it's no surprise that the brain will always look for opportunities to hand off tasks that aren't life-threatening.

One of those just happens to be something that the brain is quite literally obsessed with. In fact, the brain is so addicted to this one thing that we spend 30 per cent of our waking hours pursuing it, often without even realising it. Can you guess what it is?

It's day-dreaming.

Drifting off to far-away places, creating and experiencing fantasies, achieving or failing at the tasks we set, ultimately learning a lesson even if it really isn't clear at the time. Day-dreaming is the brain telling itself stories. The brain loves stories, it will take calculated risks, lower its guard and use energy stores to immerse itself in a story as often as it can. The brain would choose to do it all day, if only modern living wasn't getting in the way.

Day-dreaming is powerful because it's instinctive. Being instinctive means that, like eating, it is hard to resist and is the perfect plank for a marketing strategy. As marketers, communicators and business owners it would be nice to be able to enter the day-dreams of a population, strong, top of mind and desired, but most of us can't control the inner thoughts of others. However, there is an activity that stops the brain day-dreaming while providing the opportunity for smart content creators to fill the void and to do so with increased levels of concentration, focus and comprehension. That activity is *consuming* a story.

When the brain is being *fed* a story without having to do any of the work, it also relaxes and opens itself up to deeper engagement. The day-dreaming, the drifting off, stops because the storytelling work is being done for it.

Now, remember the brain has a unique ability to be incredibly selfish and as a result we see levels of concentration when engaged in a story that is able to block out external distractions. That's a unique opportunity for creators and marketers, because it increases the level and length of attention people will pay towards content that possesses story elements.

Stories via video are even more attractive to the human brain because they are the most efficient way for the brain to consume a story. It's a passive activity that takes very little energy and usually takes place in a location where it need not be on high alert for outside dangers, such as at home, on public transport, in the office ... even in the bathroom. Moving pictures move people — it's one of my rules of engagement. Video combined with sound also stimulates more parts of the brain, and the more stimulated the brain, the more it will fight to remain engaged, to the point of being disconnected from the real world.

If you have children you will know exactly the phenomenon I'm talking about. My daughters love consuming video content. Let me set the scene for you. It's Saturday morning, the smell of toast is in the air and the kids have sport to get ready for. As I walk through the lounge room they are both on the couch watching their favourite cartoons on their iPads. (Every week this happens, by the way.) I say, 'Time to get dressed — we have to leave for hockey soon.' When I come back 10 minutes later ... they haven't moved. Not a centimetre. So I stand there staring at them for a good 10 to 15 seconds (it feels like minutes). Still nothing. For a brief moment I question my existence, whether they can see or hear me at all, or have I woken up in an alternate universe? Then I deploy a tactic I learned from my mother (I was the youngest of three boys). I raise my voice. In a deeper, sterner, more urgent tone I repeat my advisory.

It works. This time I manage to break through the barriers in which their brains are holding my usually attentive and loving children hostage. They both look up at me, startled, as if I've just raised the temperature from zero to 100 without warning. Like they were genuinely shocked. Fight-or-flight responses are activated. Ms 13 runs to her room with a half-laughing squeak, while Ms 10 stays to fight. It's as though this is the first they've heard from me all morning...because in a sense it is. Their brains were locked away in stories. Parents across the planet report the same 'iPad zombie' scenario.

Well, from today you can no longer blame your children for not hearing you. You can no longer get angry with them for failing to follow your instructions. None of it is their fault. It's their brains; their attention has been hijacked. The selfish brain has put up barriers to ensure nothing and no one will interrupt their story time, their time to rest, to indulge.

This is the power of story. It has the ability not only to capture the attention of viewers but to hold it, and to do so in a way that triggers the brain to put up barriers that block out all distractions. In the noisy environment that is social media, the ability to increase concentration levels and attention while at the same time turning down the noise being made by others offers a massive advantage.

The power of long-term connection

The second superpower that story delivers has to do with connection and how it influences decisions long after your video has finished playing.

The power of a long-term connection with a viewer first comes with their ability to actually remember that you, your business or service even exist. This is particularly vital when it comes to tapping your 'half step away' market. These are potential customers who are yet to try your offering; they know about it but for some reason aren't ready to buy. The educating phase of the buyer's journey is a particularly powerful time for brands to engage and connect with potential customers.

The question is how do you increase your chances of being on their radar when it does come time to make a decision? The power of storytelling has been tested time and time again through human history. Author Christina Baldwin sums it up perfectly: 'Words are how we think…stories are how we link.' In other words, you can throw endless information at someone but that's all it is — in one ear and out the other. If you truly want to make an impact, to connect on a level that stays with them, you need to tell them a story.

Of course, how long that connection lasts depends on how good the story is. Great stories can empower the human brain to achieve incredible things. Feats most people would consider impossible or the product of some type of freak genetic imbalance. Stories allow us to remember an event in our childhood decades after. Stories allow us to recall lines from a favourite movie years later. They are powerful enough to allow humans to memorise the phonebook. (For the Millennials, you can google 'phonebook'.)

Wait. What?

Yes, you read that right. Stories are so powerful you can use them to memorise an entire phonebook. I know this because I've met and tested a guy who did it. His name is Tansel Ali and he is one of the world's leading memory experts and four-time Australian memory champion.

I first met Tansel when I was working as a TV reporter and my interest in video and viral content was still in its infancy. A chance meeting led to one of my greatest breakthroughs in understanding future trends and patterns around viral content. I was assigned to cover Tansel's attempt to recite the entire phonebook. It was a spectacular media stunt carried out by the phonebook publisher and all the pressure was on Tansel not to stuff it up.

As I watched Tansel reel off business after business listed in the directory my initial surprise soon turned to deep curiosity. How was he doing this? There were no hidden ear pieces, no secret codes hidden in the wallpaper that I could make out. I am instinctively sceptical about these types of branded stunts, let alone anyone who claims magical powers. So to test Tansel out I asked if he could recite random pages. I expected him to be a bit resistant or to set his own conditions. To my surprise, he was the opposite. Tansel said if I read him three businesses in a row from a random page he would attempt to pick up the sequence and finish the page. Of course I went deep into the phonebook, flicked backwards and forwards, a few pages here and there, in the hope of throwing him off. Then I read: *Business 1, Business 2, Business 3...*

For a moment there was silence, just the dull whirr of the camera recording... and I thought I had him.

Then Tansel came to life and reeled off the businesses on the rest of the page without a hitch. We tried it again to be sure. Again Tansel recited the rest of the page. Next I went deep into the alphabet... surely this isn't possible. Tansel delivered again with a confident grin and without a hitch.

This struck me as incredible. Little did I know that years later it would prove relevant and immensely valuable to my research.

From that day on Tansel and I would form a pretty strong friendship and eventually I thought I knew him well enough to drop the question. You don't want to be the guy who asks a magician how he performs his tricks, but this one was stuck in my brain for months and I needed to know. Finally, I summoned the courage to spit it out.

'How did you do it?'

I knew I was either going to get a no, a non-answer, a disappointing answer — or THE answer. Thankfully Tansel gave me THE answer.

He told me he remembers things by turning them into a story. Put simply, he links each of the unique names of the business and lays them down as part of an ongoing narrative, like a movie, then when prompted he just has to recall what happens next in the film he has created in his head. Having me read out a sequence of three businesses from a random page was as effective as fast forwarding Tansel's story to a certain scene, and he just picked it up from there. Tansel doesn't see himself as a freak or gifted (although there has to be something unique in his DNA); he sees himself as a storyteller. Tansel explained to me that the brain loves and holds onto great stories.

Remember, stories are a sequence of individual events retold to an audience. The brain has a way of filing the information it receives. Story structures are frameworks that match that same process so efficiently that they allow for effortless recall — increased memory. And because story structures have been time tested and refined over centuries of best practice, we know the best ones are geared towards working seamlessly with the brain, the way the brain wants to work. That seamless transfer of information increases the rate at which a viewer absorbs data, but also the rate and level at which they can comprehend, recall and even relay that information accurately to others.

Great story frameworks

If you want to tell great stories it's best to learn from the greats. Thankfully, great storytellers — from the modern entertainment industry all the way back to the oral storytellers of ancient civilisations and religions — have been studied in depth to reveal and help understand their power in connecting and influencing people. They are so time tested that most of the more effective story sequences can now be recognised and replicated. The good news is these frameworks are relatively easy to learn, but like anything the rewards lie at the other end of some solid hard work and time refining your own abilities to apply the story frameworks to your own creative ideas.

History abounds with great storytellers. Walt Disney is by far my favourite, but Shakespeare, J.K. Rowling, Steven Spielberg, George Lucas, James Cameron and tons more have also nailed it. When I think about the stories these greats have brought to life I am immediately taken back to when I first experienced them and the way they left me feeling. I can still relive the moment in my mind today and my body responds with a hint of the tingles I experienced as a kid.

Maybe you remember that feeling? You've just spent two hours in a dark cinema and as you make your way back to the foyer you emerge from the darkness, adrenaline still pumping from the journey you've been on. My mind would be filled with questions that I couldn't get out fast enough as my brothers and I relived the epic twists and turns and special effects of the adventure we'd just been on.

I've listed only a few of the storytellers who have the power to affect us in this way. But this same feeling drives the sale of toys, clothes, breakfast cereals, pot plants, sporting goods, jewellery, toothpaste, soft drinks and countless other products. The point is *you* can now also harness that power. Maybe not on a cinematic scale, but it's still yours for the taking. Across all the content you have consumed in which these greats played a hand, think about the journey they engineered, the characters they created, the variety of emotions the story provoked. In every one of these stories there are heroes and villains, adversity to be overcome, a journey and a lesson to be learned.

I will touch on just three sets of rules for storytelling. I certainly didn't invent them but I stand by their power. The upside is this: while this book and my research focus on the power of storytelling using video, the rules that dictate story are pretty universal to any medium or form. For example, the keynotes I deliver on stages around the world, and even my TED Talk, use story structures to capture the audience, hold their attention and trigger them to act. The same structures I use on my videos and even on live streams.

With the rapid emergence of new technologies around video, social media and even computer-generated special effects, it is easy to be romanced and distracted by these new tools. Yes, new and wonderful ways to communicate are being invented and launched every day: 360 video, virtual and augmented reality are great examples of how the platforms we can tell our stories on are constantly evolving. But despite the technical changes, the rules around engagement and human attention remain the same. The rules around story remain unchanged, as they have since well before humans had farms.

The Hero's Journey

Storytelling is an art. There are good ones and there are bad ones, but what you might think is good, I might think is bad. That's because our own experiences and interests shape our individual tastes. What remains consistent across most commercially made videos and in particular movies out of Hollywood is the structure in which the story is told. The sequence in which the individual events are linked.

Before you move on to the exercise, I want you to think of your favourite movie of all time. The one that you carry with you every day, reference in conversations and allow to shape your behaviour. If you don't have a recent favourite, think of a classic Disney tale from your childhood. Now, with that movie in mind, answer the following questions.

- ▶ Who is the hero?

- ▶ The villain?

- ▶ Is there a journey?

- ▶ Is there adversity?

- ▶ Was it overcome?

- ▶ Did the story end in success or failure?

- ▶ Was there a lesson?

The framework I have just laid out briefly in these questions is based on the 'Hero's Journey' story framework. It is the most popular storytelling framework in Hollywood and fast becoming popular online. It could be said that the Hero's Journey framework is responsible for holding the attention of millions of people for hours at a time as well as bringing in billions of dollars through the box office.

Imagine charging your audience to watch your content and have them paying rapt attention for 90 minutes to two hours at a time. There isn't a social media guru on the planet who would prescribe that strategy, but then again maybe there aren't that many social media gurus who truly understand the power of story and how to deploy it?

The Hero's Journey is a great story structure that when understood and mastered can be truly powerful. Just look at the videos that go viral. Videos engineered to spread always tell a story. More specifically, they contain the elements necessary for the brain to recognise the content as a vehicle with a story very early on. The immediate effect on the viewer in movies is no different from the effect story has on your kids sitting in front of a TV or iPad or a potential customer watching on their phone. It stimulates the brain and the brain puts up those barriers to block out distractions. The barriers are vital because no content can just trigger someone to take action. It takes time to generate the physical response required — in the case of viral videos, to click Share. We'll touch on how to trigger that response more deeply in the next chapter.

As I mentioned briefly in Part I, in viral videos there were two constants: the presence of story elements and the absence of selling.

And I'd seen this winning combination before. As I related in chapter 5, my very first job was as Commercial Inventory Manager at a TV station, which wasn't anywhere near as glamorous as it sounds. My job was to review and approve every TV commercial before it went to air. During those two years I was exposed to all the tricks, tactics and patterns being rolled out by advertising agencies to capture audience attention and trigger a response. Sure, I had been exposed to TV commercials before this, but day in, day out? That was a whole new level of intensity.

The problem is many advertisers believed in yelling to gain attention and offering massive discounts to trigger action. It's a tactic that hasn't stood the test of time. You only have to look at the trends on social media to understand that certain ads actually deliver a real connection, and as a result were more readily recalled, more often raised in conversation and, you guessed it, more likely to enjoy a second life as a viral video across social media. These commercials didn't yell or sell, not directly anyway. They told stories. Often the stories evolved across campaigns of numerous 30-second commercials and this left viewers eagerly awaiting the next instalment. They were playing the selfish brain, knowing it hates unresolved stories, which makes it highly receptive to tuning into the next episode to find out what happens. The Rhonda and Ketut romance campaign for Australian insurance giant AAMI is a great example of a brand using stories to camouflage actual ads.

Scan QR code to watch the video

The point is that for a number of reasons *story elements drive behaviour*, sometimes viral behaviour, sometimes buying behaviour, depending on how the story is engineered.

This was further confirmed by an analysis of 108 Super Bowl commercials. Researchers Keith Quesenberry and Michael Coolsen from Shippensburg University were looking to find what set these ads apart and made them go viral. Many found their results surprising. For instance, we are brought up to believe that 'sex sells' — look at Kim Kardashian. But is it in fact the overriding determinant of success?

Well, according to Quesenberry and Coolsen's research, there is one other factor that outstrips them all, including sex, when it comes to going viral.

Story.

'The more complete a story marketers tell in their commercials,' says Quesenberry, 'the higher it performs in the ratings polls, the more people like it, want to view it and want to share it.'

And remember not to confuse viral with being YouTube famous — viral means business.

Aristotle's three-act drama

Storytelling allows content creators to humanise a brand, create an emotional connection and also inspire or enhance a consumer's own story. There is an element of alignment between the viewer and the characters of a great story. Even if the story being depicted is fantasy or even animated, as long as the viewer can identify with the struggle or journey of the characters, a connection will be formed and that's a feeling humans find irresistible when it comes to sharing.

Throughout history there have been numerous widely adopted storytelling structures. We touched on the Hero's Journey before, but perhaps the most popular evolved from Greek philosopher Aristotle's *Poetics*, considered the earliest documented work on dramatic theory. While much of Aristotle's work in the space is lost, what survives is his observations around 'tragic' narratives.

Aristotle is credited with introducing the three-act play structure. He suggested that a play or story should present a single, whole action that is divided into three sections or 'acts' (a beginning, middle and end). Pretty simple, right? Sure, but it's what has to happen in those three 'acts' that determines the success of your narrative with an audience. Here's my simplified approach to using the three-act play framework for telling your story.

ACT 1: Start your video by identifying a problem driven by a desire that is shared by your target audience.

ACT 2: Confront and struggle with a challenge. A hero never simply knows the answers. Make it a journey of discovery.

ACT 3: End your story with success or failure. What really matters is the lesson.

Did you notice how this structure relates to elements you already identified in your belief system and when structuring your ROE? It's all connected.

In the modern media world where anyone at all can broadcast their message or story and communicate with the world, this structure is your best friend.

If you are new to content creation or you have been making videos without much success, this is the framework I suggest you start with. As popular as the Hero's Journey is in pop culture it takes work to master and I believe the three-act play is better aligned with the speed and agility that are rewarded on social media. Simple and straightforward, but still tuned into the human brain, if it wasn't so powerful we wouldn't still be talking about it so long after Aristotle's departure.

In fact, the three-act play is used by many top social media communicators. YouTubers like PewDiePie, Logan Paul and David Dobrik have videos that follow this structure. Once you become familiar with it, you will start thinking about video ideas in a three-act play format.

If you want to take things a step further, try five steps instead of three. In the mid-1800s, German novelist and playwright Gustav Freytag introduced a five-act dramatic structure. This structure remains in high use today and is associated with the 'dramatic arc' and 'Freytag's Pyramid'.

Freytag's Pyramid

1. *Exposition:* The story starts by sharing important background information with the audience. The scene is set, the main characters, their roles and personal challenges introduced. Essentially, it covers the back story.

2. *Rising action:* A series of events unfold, building towards the point of greatest interest or tension. These events are the

most important of the story as the entire plot pivots around them. They also deliver the audience to the climax.

3. *Climax:* This is the turning point that changes the main character's fate. Faced with a challenge, the main character needs to draw on inner strengths to progress. These scenes reveal the character's greatest fears or weaknesses.

4. *Falling action:* During the falling action, the protagonist is thrust into conflict with the main antagonist (bad guy). There is usually a moment of great suspense. The main character can win or lose.

5. *Denouement:* Freytag insists the audience needs to be released from any angst or tension. In the closing scenes the conflict is resolved.

As you can see, there are similarities between the dramatic structures, but even more between Freytag's Pyramid and the Hero's Journey structure.

You can download copies of all three frameworks via this QR code.

**Scan QR code
to download the
frameworks**

It's just so simple!

We now understand that brand story clarity attracts attention and that your rules of engagement keep you relevant, consistent and aligned. And also that story structures capture your viewers' attention, ensuring they watch for longer.

Walt Disney is a master storyteller who understood this inherently. He was a strong advocate of keeping stories morally simple, founded on a struggle between 'Good' and 'Evil', guaranteeing the widest audience appeal. In all his work he ensured that the characters, no matter how fanciful, were always relatable to the audience or, as he put it, 'believably personalised'. Which is the reason why generations of audiences have had a soft spot for an animated mouse who can talk. 'The moral ideals common to all humanity must be upheld,' he wrote. 'The victories must not be too easy. Strife to test valour is still and will always be the basic ingredient of the animated tale, as of all screen entertainments.'

Not only is Walt laying down the rules for excellent storytelling, but he is also adding parameters. One in particular rests on strong foundations. Viral videos are engineered on very simple, easily absorbed ideas or concepts. When Walt was first making animated movies, what he was doing was so new and intriguing that he had little trouble capturing the attention of his audience. The novelty of it helped. Fast forward to today and there's a world of distractions, attention is harder to capture and more value is placed on time. A viewer is less prepared to invest in consuming your content in the hope of it hitting the mark or becoming more interesting later. Your audience demands to be able to decipher and understand the state of play within seconds of engaging with your video. Who's the bad guy? What is the struggle? And how does it relate to them?

In the social media era it appears Freytag's first step, 'Exposition', has never been more valued. You have seconds to pique the viewer's interest while also setting the scene of the story. And this raises an interesting point around how long your videos should be. There's no shortage of gurus insisting your videos should be no more than one or two minutes long, with the acceptable duration apparently getting shorter and shorter every year all because humans are developing the attention spans of goldfish.

Have you ever sat outside a movie theatre in that dark corridor with the really squishy carpet that smells like popcorn, the one with all the cinema doors running off it? Waiting for the goldfish-headed humans to run out because they could no longer concentrate on what they were watching?

I did. I stayed for more than three minutes and *not one person left!*

Why? I was fortunate enough to explore this topic briefly with Academy Award-winning director James Cameron. I was in Hollywood for a press junket around the release of *Avatar* on Blu-ray. (Blu-ray! How quick did they get killed off?)

Anyway, I was meant to be interviewing him about how great movies like his look on Sony Blu-ray players, but for me this was a rare opportunity, one I knew would probably never come up again. These events are so tightly controlled I couldn't risk missing my chance by waiting until the end of our allotted time slot to get the answer I needed. So I opened with it. Completely out of context I asked, 'There are all these experts on social media saying videos need to be less than two minutes long because people can't concentrate for longer than that. Yet you have made billions of dollars on the back of movies that may run close to three hours. How do you keep your audience watching for such a long period of time?'

The answer didn't come straight away—just a funny, slightly puzzled look. For a moment I thought the interview was over before it had even begun. Then he leant forward in his chair with a smile and said, 'If I promise to share with you the answer at the end of today, when all the other interviews are done, would you be prepared to hang around?'

'Sure, no problem,' I responded. 'Where do you want me to wait?'

His smile grew a little before he reinforced his point. 'No, that's the answer. If I promise to share with you the answer at the end of today, when all the other interviews are done, would you be prepared to hang around?'

James Cameron was establishing the foundations of a story in my brain, using the promise of a lesson at the end of a long wait, the journey, which I would have to experience to reach that moment of success or failure. He opened a loop that my inquisitive brain was prepared to hang around to close.

Successful movies, TV shows, internet videos, along with authors and performers, deploy this tactic to buy time from their viewers, to get them to invest in the story in order to close a loop, meanwhile buying the creators time to help them catch feelings.

When pressed on their goldfish theory, the gurus will tell you they are basing their conclusion on hard data. Quoting falling average watch time statistics, they interpret them to prove people are watching less. Because we are so busy and social media is so noisy, we are just skipping through videos and not watching them right through. This could be a sound argument if not for the fact that video consumption is higher than ever. More people are watching video and more people are making and publishing video. There's also that crazy YouTube statistic that eight hours of video is uploaded every second.

But guess what? Ninety-nine per cent of the video content is either really crap or simply irrelevant to you. They don't have the ingredients to hook and hold your attention, and certainly don't employ addictive story frameworks. As a result, watch times are decreasing but it is because consumers are becoming more selective and at the same time less prepared to work hard to find the videos they want. I call it the *abandonment effect*. It's not that viewers' attention span is shorter; it's that they are spoilt for choice. Now the power is in their hands, they're more protective of their time. That makes them less likely to waste time on videos that don't serve them well, that don't hook them with a story loop right from the start or that are just marginally too complicated to be comprehended.

Our brains consume and recall the simple stuff, which is also easier to share. How many times have you watched a clever commercial or viral video and thought, 'Wow, that's brilliant!' More often than not when I have those moments what I am really thinking is, 'That was such a great idea. Why didn't I think of it? It's just so simple.'

My research indicates that simple stories are more widely shared, and it makes perfect sense considering that by sharing a piece of content you are effectively giving it your stamp of approval. The key consideration is the lesson or 'moral' of the story. What does it tell us? If the lesson is complex and difficult to understand or requires extra brain capacity or even assumed prior knowledge to sort out, chances are most people will err on the side of caution and won't risk sharing it.

tip

It is way too easy to make yourself the hero of your own stories. And a big mistake. Like the story itself, you are the bridge or guide that assists your viewers to transform. Your viewers, your audience, your potential customers — make them the heroes. #behumble

In a noisy social media world, brands are already demanding a lot from people by urging them to consume their content. An even bigger ask is to have them lock your message away in their memory banks, so listen to Walt and reduce the friction points by keeping all your stories simple.

Another of Walt Disney's pillars of successful storytelling is his ability to take viewers on a 'ride'. Using skilled storytelling techniques, Disney and his studio of talented creators had the power to make thousands of people laugh and cry in a matter of minutes in the same story. That's how deep and real the connections are. How and why did Disney blaze this trail? That leads us directly into the next chapter.

recap:
THE BRIDGE

- Thinking brains don't act, feeling brains do. If you want them to share, you first have to get them to care.

- Stories are the bridge that transforms a thinking brain into a feeling brain.

- The brain is the most selfish organ in the human body; play to it.

- Stories increase the rate of memory recall.

exercise:
DESIGNING A SIMPLE STORY

Let's design a simple story in the 'three-act play' framework. Remember, being simple doesn't mean it's less powerful. In fact, our research puts the three-act play at the top of the ladder for social content and the ability to trigger engagement. Being simple also allows you to be nimble, reacting and responding quickly.

ACT I

In Act I you need to communicate to the audience that there's a problem, that you have the ability and desire to solve that problem, and what is at stake if you fail to solve it. It is vital that your audience can visualise or connect with the person with the problem.

In point form, set down your first act.

- _____
- _____
- _____

ACT II

This is where the character/ person moves through the challenge of solving the problem. It cannot be easy. You don't simply stumble across the answer to a great problem-solving story. It's a journey that highlights the frustrations and failures your audience could expect or may have already experienced when trying to solve the problem.

In point form, write down your second act.

- _____
- _____
- _____

ACT III

With the journey coming to a close, there has to be a point of realisation. Did you solve the problem? Was the journey a success or a failure? Many people think that only stories that end with success are themselves a success. It's not true. Your story can end in success or failure; what is important when it comes to Like, Comment, Share, Buy activity is the lesson. What is the lesson of your story?

In point form, write down your third act.

- _____

- _____

- _____

chapter 10
emotional buy-in

Ever cried at the movies? Offered someone a heartfelt hug of reassurance during an engaging TV show? Jumped out of your seat with excitement while watching a sports match? Shared a favourite video with others online? These are common enough experiences in our media-drenched society. What you may not realise is that all these very human responses to content are linked. In fact, studying these everyday interactions tells us a lot about why people share and how you do it yourself.

Why do people share?

This is the question that triggered my own explorations, the mystery to which I ended up spending five years of my life. I'm honoured to be able to share with you my conclusions.

In my journey to uncover the secret sauce to spreadable videos, I found I had to ask myself another, slightly different question. Why do people cry when watching movies? Like really cry, real tears...watching a fictional movie. I mean, no one really died, for goodness' sake — they're actors! Sometimes they're even cartoons that people are bawling their eyes out over.

When you think about it logically, realistically, it doesn't make sense, but when you block off the thinking brain and let feelings take over ...

Think about how Apple markets the iPhone. There are plenty of cheaper phones on the market that do almost exactly the same things as the iPhone. But Apple has made us feel differently about its products, to the point where people will camp out on the street for a week to be one of the first to get their hands on the latest model. If they came back a week later they could simply walk into the store and buy the very same phone, in and out in a few minutes, but there's kudos in being among the first to own the new model. Again, logic doesn't come into it.

The mechanism that the brain possesses and activates when it is locked in a story, the one that allows your kids to constantly ignore you, is incredibly influential. Not only does it block out the distractions, but it plays a second important role in transitioning a viewer from being alert to being invested. What I call 'the shift' is actually the brain transitioning from its regimented thinking mode to its emotional feeling mode. And the reason this change is important when it comes to viral videos and messaging is that only a feeling brain shares or likes or cries or, more importantly, buys.

So let's explore that.

The shift

We've studied the process of engaging the human brain, and grabbing and holding its attention. Now we change the focus to the art of achieving buy-in, culminating in the moment when it decides whether to take action, the brain flicking a switch to trigger a physical response.

The biggest influence on that decision is, hands down, not how we think but how we feel. We are taught from a young age how to think, how to solve puzzles, how to ask and answer questions, and make decisions, but feelings are instinctive. Which means they can often seem nonsensical or even irrational. It's an observation we need to remind ourselves of more often: *Humans don't think, they feel.*

All the great storytellers, from Shakespeare to Disney, understood this. Now we are seeing smart brands and even individuals executing on this advanced understanding as the hood is lifted on the secrets to successful performance and video production. Disney said, 'I'm just corny enough to like to have a story hit me over the heart.' Part of Disney's storytelling formula was to have children cry as much as they laugh. His aim was to trigger as wide a range of feelings as he could, because then more parts of the brain light up and deeper connections are developed.

Viral videos are also fuelled by feelings. Great videos emerge from the noise because of emotions. To push an audience's emotional buttons you have to know and understand them.

Having the audience cry during a movie is fairly common, but have you noticed how it never happens in the opening scene? This is because the audience needs time to invest in the characters and the story.

If you kill off a character in the opening scene of a movie the emotional response is typically low, because no one knows enough about the character to care much. The level of physical response, whether laughter or tears or sharing, is dictated by the level of emotional buy-in.

The process that occurs in the brain that triggers you to cry when watching a movie is the same process that happens in your brain to trigger a Like, Comment, Share or even a Buy after watching a video. Emotions play a significant role in the video consumption process. You can't watch a video and not have an emotional response to it; you must be feeling something. If a movie can make you cry, a video can make you Like, Comment, Share or Buy.

Among videos that exhibit all the elements associated with the Spread Factor, Dove Sketches is a great example of how emotions play a starring role in triggering a response. But before you dive in and watch I want you to prepare yourself to be open to what it is this video has to offer. This may be strange for those of you on a plane or train, or even sitting by a pool at your favourite resort, but please follow along as best you can.

First get your headphones sorted so you don't have to wrestle with them and miss the start of the video. Then take your left hand and touch the left side of your nose. Now draw a line with your finger down your face and chest until you reach the centre of your chest at about nipple height. (If you are over 50, where your nipples used to be. Lol.) Your finger should be sitting just on the edge of your left pectoral muscle near your heart. This is where you feel. I want you to concentrate on the changes that occur in this area of your body while you're watching this video.

**Scan QR code
to watch the
video**

This video obviously targets Dove's core demographic, women aged 35 plus. Even if you don't sit in that demographic, we have confirmed that this video will still have an effect. It moves people. Did you feel it? In terms of Spread Factor ratings, the Virable formula is consistently returning scores around 98–100. Remember, anything over a score of 80 on the Virable formula is likely to be shared 87 per cent of the time. In terms of triggering a response, this video is nothing less than a rocket.

So let's break it down into the stages we have worked through so far. The first hurdle this video jumps is gaining attention. It does that, in my opinion, by placing the forensic artist in the scene right at the beginning. That generates instant intrigue as our brain tries to work out why he is there. Importantly, the forensic artist provides one other very vital element. He starts telling us his story. So in the initial seconds your brain is immediately intrigued. But while you are still trying to make sense of the scene the video is doing something clever. In the time it takes for your brain to assess what is going on, it is hijacked by the artist starting to tell his story. In rapid succession the video then initiates multiple stories, and opens multiple story loops, by introducing the women whose faces are being sketched. Those women clearly represent the feelings and desires of the core demographic, which makes it highly relevant to them, and within the opening scenes the viewers that count to Dove are raising their distraction-proof barriers and starting to wind down their thinking brains. Feelings start changing into strong emotions, buy-in takes place and it's only a matter of seconds before the physical response trigger is instinctively switched.

It's quite a ride, and it debunks many theories and approaches being peddled by marketing 'experts'. The biggest myth is around a set duration for videos. The number one question I am asked is, 'How long should a video be?' My answer to that question, given everything I know, is, 'As long as it takes to trigger the physical response you're chasing.' If you are after watch time to improve your standings with a social platform's algorithm, then the answer becomes, 'As long as you can hold their attention.'

Did you notice how the emotions in the Dove video build up over time? It's no surprise to me that there are three distinct 'acts' that work to develop the emotional buy-in required for success. This video is also a great example of how context really counts. I find this video so much more powerful now that I have two daughters. Their arrival in my life has awakened my conscience in areas I need to know more about in order to be a 'tuned-in' dad and to protect them. Where I am in my life changes how I relate to women and girls and all the issues they confront in the modern world. As a result, it changes the contextual position I'm in when I watch videos like this one.

You may also have noticed that by simply being engaged with this book and having me request that you watch it, your brain is less resistant to the risks. As with the power of sharing, I validated that this video was worth watching, that it offered a valuable lesson or lessons. I was careful not to mention that Dove Sketches is one of the most successful viral brand videos ever made or that it recorded the highest Spread Factor score we have ever encountered.

The point I want to make about this video is the power it has over our emotions, the main element in content consumption and the subsequent response. No matter what you are watching or reading, your brain, indeed your entire being, is calculating and emotionally reacting to it. Content and emotions go hand in hand. If you're engaging with a piece of content you are having feelings about it. If you are feeling nothing then I have some bad news ... you need to check your pulse.

The single most important lesson I learned about what makes people share came from studying this video. I had just started researching the science of viral phenomena full time when this video was at the peak of its power. It was the most talked about and analysed video by researchers, social scientists, human behaviour specialists, psychologists, women's affairs lobbyists, advertising experts and, most importantly, everyday women.

Primary emotions

Dove are not the first brand to create a video that tugs at the heartstrings or makes you reflect on how you are living your life. Walt Disney had been doing this with famous fairy tales for decades. What Disney and Dove are tapping into is our physiological responses to certain emotions. Emotions dictate physical, instinctive responses in humans. But when it comes to which responses are triggered ... not all emotions are created equal.

There are 17 primary emotions I focus on when assessing how a human being is feeling while consuming content. They are, in no particular order:

- happiness
- surprise
- disgust
- irritation
- calmness
- discomfort
- frustration
- hilarity
- awe
- anger
- shock
- boredom
- amusement
- exhilaration
- inspiration
- astonishment
- sadness

I'm sure you can all think of times in your life when you have experienced each of these emotions. Hopefully you aren't experiencing number 12 while reading this book. (Hey, I know you went back and counted. ☺)

To understand why people share different emotions at different rates, it's important first to understand how the emotions are actually different from each other and how they exist in relation to each other. This is done by dividing the 17 emotions into groups based on two variables: positive vs negative, and strong vs weak.

Emotions deliver us a positive or negative assessment of what we are consuming. There are videos that leave you happy and others that leave you sad. We already know that part of Walt Disney's formula for the perfect movie was to have as many moments of tears as there are moments for laughs. He did this to stimulate as many emotions as possible, almost like a rollercoaster effect to keep the audience locked inside the story he was telling. One important point to note is that Disney always left them happy, and there's a good reason for this.

This approach reveals the benefits of building the Spread Factor and why it is critical to video marketing success. We associate laughter with being happy and crying with being sad but the truth is by the time the human body initiates a physical response of laughter or tears we have actually moved beyond being just happy or sad. Our feeling brains have essentially tapped a higher level of emotions. A strong emotional response triggers an equally strong physical response. These heightened physical responses are what control or trigger a person to take action. So you need to target the strong emotions, not the passive feelings, if you want success.

The reach and influence of a video lives and dies online according to the emotional response it evokes. For starters, emotions that are classified as weak don't trigger any physical response — no interaction, not even negative feedback. This category includes emotions like *bored* and *calm*. The viewer may watch these videos to garner particular information but they won't be driven to act, as they would with strong emotions that often trigger a response before the video has even ended. The measurable difference between strong and weak emotions when it comes to interactions is on average a factor of five.

So when you are developing creative ideas for your content you need to consider the emotional response the idea will generate as potentially just as important as whether it is relevant enough to sit within your rules of engagement and whether it aligns with your overall belief system.

But targeting strong emotions is only part of the equation. Breaking the process down one step further reveals that within the strong emotions category you have both positive and negative feelings, and these project their own influences over instinctive human responses and behaviours. In other words, positive and negative emotions from the 'strong' category cause viewers to act very differently.

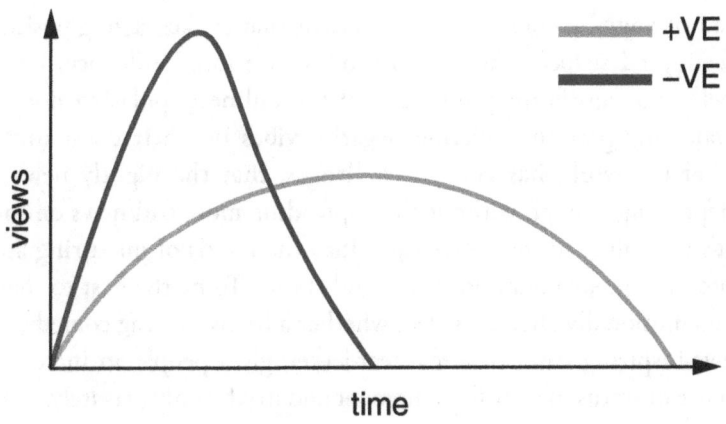

Consider this graph. Negative emotions that trigger strong responses such as *anger* and *sadness* are what I call fast movers. They are shared around at a high rate in a short time. This means they peak very early on. They spike. Their reach is deep, the energy around them is electric but their life span is short. They might be compared to road rage. A car cuts you off in traffic, like a real jerk move. It gets you wound up, and you respond by raising your hand or barking a choice epithet, maybe even flashing your headlights. At the next intersection the offending driver turns left while you continue on straight. You may offer one last disapproving shake of the head but essentially now that car is no longer around you your emotional investment pretty quickly returns to neutral. That's the life cycle of a viral video triggered by strong negative feelings.

Videos fuelled by strong positive emotions have a very different life cycle.

Humorous content is by far the most popular online material but there is also a lot more of it, which makes it a crowded category where you'll find a lot more and stronger competition. Positive content that we find hilarious, exhilarating or that leaves us in awe isn't shared as feverishly as strong negative content that leaves us angry despite the emotional response still being a strong one.

Is the frenzy around rapidly sharing strong negative content driven by scarcity, because we don't come across content that makes us sad or angry as often as we do content that evokes strong positive feelings? I suspect 'short supply' does have some influence. I also believe a significant proportion of the online population doesn't want any part in inflicting negative vibes on their community. That the world has enough challenges, that the nightly news is depressing enough without their spreading more bad news online. It's an influence that plays right into the hands of nurturing and protecting our reputations, ego and status. To be the first to share an emotionally charged video, whether a barnstorming comedy, an awe-inspiring stunt or a real tear-jerker, gives people an increased sense of status, if only for a moment and maybe only privately.

Among my Facebook friends, as I've mentioned, my gold ticket is finding and sharing *Star Wars*-related posts. Being the first to deliver and share these clips makes me feel as if I am improving my status among my friends because I'm more 'in tune' with *Star Wars* than them, making me the mega-fan of the group. I even feel uncomfortable writing those lines because it seems so trivial but it's an honest observation of real behaviour. The flow-on effect is the connection I have just made with the page or person who brought that video to my attention. They provided me with the opportunity to build a small amount of prestige by providing the post or video I shared. They are my supplier, so they would have to work hard in the wrong direction to have me unlike or unfollow them. That buys them time to build connection, trust and perhaps, if they want, drive a sale.

When it comes to overall reach, there isn't a clear winner between strong positive and strong negative content, only life span. When it comes to sheer numbers there are examples of both that have amassed vast numbers of views — in the hundreds of millions.

Some online commentary suggests *happy* videos are more likely to go viral, but it's not what I see from the data collected using the Virable formula. In terms of frequency, number of views, audience size and reach they are very similar. What differs is the rate or time frame in which those views are achieved. As described, a strong negative video attracts views like a steep mountain, a road-raging burst of energy that quickly dissipates. Meanwhile strong positive videos gather their views at a steadier rate. They take their time traversing the internet until they reach their peak then slide down the other side at a similar rate.

I rank the emotions and their propensity to trigger a human to share in the following groups. And the key to triggering these feelings always circles back to context. Being clear around your brand story, being consistent within your rules of engagement, knowing how to hijack attention with story structures then triggering the right emotional response.

1. Biggest response:

- ► hilarity
- ► awe
- ► anger
- ► sadness
- ► exhilaration.

These are by far the most active emotions. If you look up any hugely successful viral video it will provoke at least one of these emotions. If it doesn't, double check the video's context and key demographic (you may not find it funny if it wasn't made for you). If you are seeking to create a weapon of mass consumption, without at least one of these emotions being triggered by your content, your viral dreams will struggle.

2. Not bad:

- ► inspiration
- ► surprise
- ► happiness
- ► shock.

Creating content that triggers these emotions doesn't mean they won't spread — they certainly will. The journey may be a little slower than others but these emotions are still very powerful. The key to this group is to aim to combine them to add extra *oomph* and increase the Spread Factor score of your videos.

3. Need help:

- disgust

- irritation

- astonishment

- amusement.

Now we are starting to get into the emotional states we want to avoid as content creators. These emotions are in the low-stimulant category, which means you are going to struggle to generate a physical response or action from the viewer. To have your content driving results you have to motivate them to react. The most common reason content lands in this category, provoking these emotions, is that you decided to play it safe. You have to understand that the internet and social networks don't need any more bad, lacklustre content. There is that much of it being made that no one is going to miss it if you don't add to the pile. You can find literally billions of videos with fewer than 100 views in the deep, dark, forgotten chasm of YouTube or Facebook Watch. You can't aim to go viral then choose to play it safe. The two simply don't go together. Worse still, if you keep producing and publishing unexceptional, unstimulating content, where you're taking up someone's most precious commodity — their time — and not getting a response, you will lose them forever.

And before we move on to the final group let's talk about *disgust*.

Out of these four emotions, disgust doesn't provoke many shares for a slightly different reason from the others. While *irritation*, *astonishment* and *amusement* do make you feel something, it's not enough to trigger a physical response in most people. Disgust works in a different way, and it's personal. Social media platforms generally reflect or document our lives, so most people are aware enough to evaluate what they post before they post it. Disgust does provoke a significant physical response. Disgust can trigger crying, fist banging; it can cause people to cover their eyes and even walk out of a room. *But* disgust is very rarely a feeling people want to be associated with, especially as a purveyor of it. Disgust is an understandable anomaly in what we see taking place on social media. When someone likes or follows you, there is a connection and a trust in that relationship. If one of your friends starts posting content you find disgusting, it's likely some of your other friends will also find it disgusting. You don't want to be the one responsible for spreading it into your network. Avoid disgust at all costs.

The final group of emotions include:

4. Avoid:

- ▶ calmness

- ▶ discomfort

- ▶ frustration

- ▶ boredom.

The fact no one shares content that triggers these emotions makes sense when spelt out in a book like this but I'm still amazed how many videos that sit in this category are still posted online, particularly videos made by big-budget brands. It's as if they haven't even assessed their own experiences and behaviours when consuming content on social media. The challenge is this: you may think the content you're making is awe-inspiring yet your audience considers it boring. In my 20 years' experience in TV, video and content production, I can't say I've ever set out to make content that makes people feel any of these emotions, but I can guarantee I've made content that has triggered them. Now, it would be easy for me to write them off as 'Everyone has a bad day', and trust me when I say I've had many and I know I still have more left in me.

The key is never to take an 'L': never let an underperforming video be a loss. Social media is a data-rich environment where even bad videos can teach you something. And this is where the Virable formula comes full circle. If your audience isn't responding to your content the way you are, one of two things is wrong. Either you are targeting the wrong audience or you aren't making the right content for those who follow you. That takes us back to the brand story and being really clear, not about who you think you are, but about *what you are to your audience*. And if you are struggling to attract any kind of audience at all, then I suspect it goes beyond simply not being clear about your story to actually not taking a strong enough stand for an audience to buy into. Be purpose based.

Out of the four emotions in this bottom bracket, *calmness* stands alone as the only one of the group on the positive axis. Calmness by its very nature is about lowering the energy in the human body, reducing the instinctive responses and taking time to respond to ... nothing. To trigger a response from this mindset is counterintuitive. Creating calmness sits most notably in the mindfulness and health space, and the actions come from external recommendations and referrals, not during the participation, consumption period. For example, if you are consuming meditation videos on YouTube, normally you would complete the experience and get on with your day — no liking, no commenting, just floating forward into what life has to offer.

A moment of peak relevance usually occurs after you mention you are meditating and someone in your filter bubble wants to know more or to try it, at which point you share the video guidance you trust. This is very different from blasting something out into your feeds in a way that fuels the viral cycle. Emotions like *discomfort*, *frustration* and *boredom* are red flags that you are doing something very wrong or missing something very important in your videos. In fact, you are entering into an area that could result in damage to your brand and reputation if you let it ride too long.

Knowing your audience and setting boundaries in your rules of engagement should mean you avoid making your target audience feel uncomfortable. Discomfort can often mark the early stages of disgust, so be very careful. Frustration is often the result of the content not being aligned or even native to the platform. For example, posting eight separate videos to Instagram to deliver a four-minute video would be very frustrating. Don't laugh, I've seen it done and yes it worked: I was left feeling very frustrated. Use IGTV for the longer format, with Instagram working as a trailer to draw people in and 'sell the story'.

Frustration can also come from the physical presentation of a piece of content, such as zero regard for the context in which the content is going to be consumed, how it is going to be consumed and the possible hurdles that may delay the actual consumption. Mobile is the main device for consuming content, yet so many brands don't optimise for it. They make a piece of content and post it as widely as they can, hoping to get as many hits as possible. Often this involves cross-pollinating across social platforms — something the platforms themselves hate — and as a result they will make the experience a clunky, difficult one. Posting a YouTube video link on Facebook is easily the most recognisable example of this. Don't do it.

To avoid frustration, plan from the start, envisage the exact scenario where and when the content is going to be consumed, think of the distractions and challenges, and plan for them. Strategically remove any barriers that could lead to friction, so all your viewers have to worry about is getting lost in your story.

Killers vs Enablers

So now you know that the key to triggering the viral response is first to create a powerful emotional response. You are also aware that there are plenty of hurdles to clear before you get the chance to make and hold a connection that will allow an emotionally triggered response.

In viral videos there is a constant battle between what I call *emotion killers* and *emotion enablers*.

Enablers

Emotion enablers enhance the experience. They make the hairs on the back of your neck stand up and gives you goose bumps.

Music and cinematography are by far the most powerful emotion-enabling tools. Music can either lift or lower the mood of a video. We see it in movies all the time, when we could turn off the dialogue and consume the music within the film and still know what is happening. For example, music that matches the action and mood will help you pace your dialogue and even your edits.

Humans are visual learners and cinematography is about making video pictures an art form. It's not vital but it can definitely help. The key is to choose the effects and filters that enhance the emotion you are targeting.

Whether shooting in a studio or in a room, your lighting too should reflect the emotions you are aiming to trigger. This is because the brain takes signals and data from the entire environment. It's why videos about homelessness are never filmed indoors and usually take place at night, the time of day when most people desire being inside, safe and protected. This is because the brain gathers and computes this information to build context and make decisions around how it handles the information it is retrieving. How that information is translated then leads to the formation of feelings.

Silence is perhaps the most underutilised enabler on the internet. In such a noisy environment, silence has become incredibly powerful. Use it to your advantage, allowing your viewers to breathe, buy into the experience and become emotionally charged.

Real, relevant and relatable

Much like the Dove videos, if you can get your audience to picture themselves in the scenario playing out on their screens then the emotional buy-in will increase significantly. This buy-in will deliver greater actions and greater reach.

Understand that social media is the new reality TV. To be real, relevant and relatable you have to create your content the way your audience would create theirs. Big brands struggle with this because they often rely on ad agencies to create not only their ads but also their content. As a result, much of the content they put out is overproduced, sanitised and picture perfect. If all you have is your phone, it's going to be hard to match, so purely through the way in which the brand has delivered its content they have created a disconnect with the real people they were trying to reach.

Remember, social media is a place to connect on a human level, so understand your videos don't have to be perfect; in fact, I would encourage you to make sure they aren't. If you are a brand on social media you need to humanise your approach. You are now sitting in a newsfeed with family members and friends, so act like it.

The only time 'fake' works in a video is when it is so well orchestrated that the actual debate about whether it is real or not fuels the Likes, Comments and Sharing. In fact, in some corners of the internet the debate still rages. This video by clothing brand Ecko is a classic example.

Scan QR code to watch the video

Killers

Emotion killers are essentially times or moments that disconnect a viewer from the story sequence. Here are a few more common examples of action killers.

▶ **Tech.** It can be things like bad audio (like fingernails on a chalkboard, humans can't bear bad audio), slow load time, buffering during playback, mid-roll ads, even messages and calls when you are watching content on your phone. Remember when phones were for making calls? Now we get upset if someone rings us on them. All of these issues disconnect the viewer from what they're consuming. Remember that the connection is fragile and while the storytelling walls can block out distractions, they can't preclude tech issues.

▶ **Schizophrenic storytelling.** This is a massive issue on livestreaming but is also common on traditional videos. Your audience has clicked onto a video because it is relevant to a desire they have. If you stop serving that desire by jumping around to different topics, your audience will become less engaged and as a result less emotionally attached. The viewer's brain will take up a defensive position to avoid any risks rather than leaning into the experience and allowing themselves to get lost in your story.

▶ **Swearing.** I know this is going to cause a ton of people to tweet me a link to Gary Vee's Monday motivation video, but hear me out on this one. Swearing *can* be a killer if your audience isn't expecting it. With Gary, it doesn't take long for you to work out what you are going to get in terms of the language he uses. I love the guy and credit him with getting me started on this journey back in 2012. He is the first to admit that swearing has cost him followers and business. But he says it's a price he's prepared to pay to remain 'real, relevant and relatable', which is an interesting trade-off.

On the platform side of things, Facebook and YouTube are now actively throttling videos that use explicit language or touch on Not Safe for Work topics. In fact, YouTube is now striking creators who swear or bully others. So your channel is turned down or restricted, and if you offend three times you are struck off the platform.

- **Selling.** I'm all for selling because it's where the money comes from, but when it comes to video it just doesn't always fly. You need to be very strategic about how and when you sell and also be prepared to pay the algorithm-issued penalty for a low-response video. You can do it — I do. But I don't do it all the time and I make sure when I do sell via my videos that I go all in. Because ultimately if you are going to pay a price you may as well make it worthwhile. Beyond trying to sell a course or a product, selling yourself in your videos is another big killer. Remember, it's not about you but about what you can do for your audience. It's best to let your actions and information do the selling. Take a stand and watch your followers join you on your journey.

recap:
EMOTIONAL MOTIVATION

- If a movie can make you cry, you can make a video that has people Like, Comment, Share and Buy.

- Humans don't think, they feel.

- Don't predetermine the running length of your video. It should be as long as you can hold their attention and trigger them to act.

- Aim to provoke a strong response through both positive and negative emotions.

chapter 11
triggered

Don't aim to make yourself the conversation, aim to put yourself in the conversation.

We're all familiar with the term 'trigger finger'. Well, a modern-day behavioural change is redefining it. Leaving the six-shooters and the Wild West behind, triggers are reminders or connections to already stored pieces of information or established knowledge that do exactly as the word suggests: they trigger us to recall, think or talk about a topic, situation or experience. Whether it's a scene from a movie, a life experience, a particular name (insert name of the first person you kissed), a brand, a video you watched or even a place, our life journey is a collection of memories. Triggers are reminders to open up those memory files so we can share our experiences at appropriate times.

Triggers are also handy when it comes to helping build a greater knowledge base or understanding of a topic we already have a history with. Say you grew up fascinated by Lego, that thought alone will take you back to a childhood of carefree creativity and remembering your favourite build. Fast forward to life as an adult, you'll probably not be thinking about Lego as much as you used to, but if it truly brought you the opportunity to escape creatively, then your brain won't have forgotten; in fact, it will be subconsciously on the lookout for triggers linked to Lego that will allow you to reopen that memory file. Once it is front and centre it is available for you to use, to share as a story or a level of knowledge or even to reminisce and ensure you are engaged in whatever conversation may be taking place on the topic of Lego. Your past experience invites you to be part of the current conversation.

Understanding this very simplified version of how a very complex organ in the human body operates is important when it comes to creating content, particularly content you want people to share.

Humans are hungry beasts. We are increasingly hungry for social media content. And with time and sophistication the human trigger is becoming more sensitive to trusted pieces of information. You already have an understanding of context and a profile of your audience, and you know the stories that will keep you relevant as a brand and the emotions that will drive your message forward. The next step, which will amplify your efforts exponentially, is setting the triggers.

Setting the triggers

Triggers take many forms. I'm currently fascinated by the interaction between street art and augmented reality and how it is pushing the boundaries of digital technology to enhance storytelling. The influence it has on humans can be as practical as changing the way they move around city streets through to lead generation and data collection. As audiences are divided off into ever more niche groups, marketing strategy continues to evolve, thanks to the increased levels of data captured on individuals. This data allows creators to be smarter when it comes to targeting triggers. But for now let's remain focused on mass market influence.

Videos that produce mass reactions either start a wave or ride a wave. Either way they always capture the Zeitgeist (mood or spirit) of a community at a particular moment. Many variables can influence the mood of a community, even the context of their understanding around particular issues and opinions.

The main categories that help shape and define those variables (particularly in Western societies) are:

- ▶ pop culture
- ▶ news/events
- ▶ seasons/holidays
- ▶ trending/hashtags
- ▶ music.

One constant across all of these categories is the Zeitgeist and the role it plays in influencing thinking and what is topical. Whether they are trying to *go viral* by creating something no one has ever seen before or are planning to take a topic or trend to a place it has never been before, the Zeitgeist is pivotal. Even YouTubers like PewDiePie and Casey Neistat speak about the power and influence of the societal mood in their creative process. One way of looking at it is picking the trends. Creating videos that are advancing or picking up on emerging trends. A lot of it comes down to timing. Too early and the mass market won't be invested enough to understand or care. Too late and the moment could well have passed and you'll be considered out of touch.

So how do you tune into the Zeitgeist? The answer is you 'live it'. You need to immerse yourself in the environment your audience occupies and experience their lifestyle first-hand.

Pop culture

Want your content to pop? You'd better add some culture. Pop culture defines generations, from Hip Hop music to *Star Wars*. If you know someone's age, you have a very real chance of triggering their interests based on pop culture trends. Injecting pop culture triggers is by far the most important move to achieve mass exposure and to accelerate emotional buy-in.

Incorporating elements of pop culture fast-tracks the processes of establishing your position in the marketplace and building trust. By making a connection to an ideal, attitude or interest a significant proportion of the audience already holds, you'll be seen as like-minded and will be more rapidly trusted. As a result, the barriers to entry will be lowered and your audience's focus will be heightened, at least in the early stages.

There is probably no better example of what an injection of the right type of pop culture can do for a piece of content than the Volvo Trucks Epic Split video where nineties action hero Jean-Claude Van Damme performs the splits between two moving vehicles. The video went on to be the most viewed viral brand video of the year, with Volvo celebrated for its audacious approach to social media rather than traditional channels. You can watch the video via QR code below, if you haven't seen it yet.

Scan QR code to watch the video

What most people don't know about the Volvo campaign is that the Van Damme video was just one of a series. The first handful went largely unnoticed despite their pulling stunts like burying one of Volvo's senior engineers up to his head and driving a truck straight over the top in an effort to demonstrate the clearance distances of the truck's undercarriage. In another, titled 'The Ballerina', high-liner

Faith Dickey walks a tightrope between two moving trucks. Don't get me wrong, both were awesome videos with significant attraction and shareability engineered into them. These videos, by their very nature, deserved a way greater response than they received. Only once they introduced the pop culture figure Van Damme did the Volvo campaign draw the widespread attention it deserved. Van Damme was the trigger.

Why it took off so significantly is based on a number of elements. At the time social networks were maturing, with massive growth in the 35+ demographic, and while the internet is drowning in content, pieces targeting this demographic weren't at saturation levels. This age group were teenagers or in their early twenties when Van Damme was in his Hollywood prime. The context of Van Damme being an action movie hero who performed his own stunts pulled a massive online trigger. Action movie lovers across the internet rejoiced in sharing the awe-inspiring video that, combined with prior knowledge and encased in Van Damme's celebrity, came together to form an awesome story. The success of this video not only triggered memories and conversations and I'm sure that 'leaving the movies' adrenaline tingle, but also increased the number of downloads of old Van Damme movies.

This video also did one more thing: it helped Volvo transition their brand. In the eighties and nineties the running joke, at least here in Australia, around bad drivers was contained in the catchline 'Bloody Volvo drivers', with their lawn bowls hat on the back sill, their big brick chassis, slow speed and all the extras. Volvo was an old-person brand built on safety and quality engineering. The one thing Volvo wasn't was daring or exciting, and they certainly weren't cool. Now the Van Damme video didn't reverse all that but it did add precision, risk and excellence to the Volvo brand story. While the stunts involved trucks, the cool factor flows across the entire brand. Add the context that the videos were only online, and all of a sudden Volvo is a brand that understands modern consumers, maybe even nudging 'cool', but certainly on the radar after delivering content the core audience wants, in the format they want it and with a powerful trigger that invites people to interact.

Scan QR code to watch the video

News/events

News and events can provide a significant boost to the earlier launch phase of viral videos. The two work in very different ways but are equally powerful tactics to adopt if they are available. Recently in Melbourne, where I live, a group of urban explorers who post their adventures on YouTube came across the carcass of a Great White shark abandoned in an old wildlife park.

For a number of weeks the videos did the rounds on YouTube, gathering momentum and attention for the creators. As their popularity grew, so did the number of 'explorers' who headed to the site to get shots of this incredible find. But while the videos were attracting views at a steady rate, they only really went viral once the discovery hit the mainstream news. YouTubers such as Jay Boston enjoyed significant growth in both subscribers and millions of views on the back of the mainstream attention. In fact, I have become friends with Jay as a result, and even months later he is still enjoying the benefits of a video that has popped on the back of a mass market trigger.

Seeding the content to audiences outside of social media seems counterintuitive to any of us who are social media converts, but ultimately attention is attention. And while the influence of mainstream media is in retreat, they still have the ability to bring a surge of viewers in a short amount of time. Especially now those still watching TV do so with one eye on the phone, right there in their hand.

Events are equally influential in triggering the viral sequence. I classify events as organised gatherings of people with a similar interest. These can be formal or informal; the common denominator is that most of those involved are driven by the same interest or desire. This means they should also be sharing the same challenges and seeking the same experiences. Whether it's a sporting event, a protest or even a conference, an opportunity exists for you to garner exponentially more attention to your content by targeting a like-minded audience.

Crafting videos to trigger these desires will come from ensuring you fully understand the reason they are there and what they are seeking from the experience. Create the video that is going to trigger the greatest emotive response in this moment of peak relevance. Seed it to the audience, or even a fraction of the audience, via an event hashtag or handle or by holding conversations in the social containers that exist and your video, if it contains the right story elements, will start to spread.

Seasons/holidays

Are you struggling for creative ideas? Never seem to have enough content for your schedule? Did you know that most viral videos are triggered by seasons and holidays? The calendar is by far the easiest and richest hunting ground for launching viral videos. If you're struggling for ideas, simply grab a calendar and work your way through the different seasonal festivities. The time of year has a massive influence on the Zeitgeist. As long as your brand story is clear and your ROEs are in place it will be easy to find a creative angle strong enough to deliver your Viral DNA to your audience. Think Christmas, New Year's, Valentine's Day, Mother's Day, Father's Day, Halloween, Summer, Winter, Autumn and Spring... the list goes on. Each brings a spike in internet traffic and interest. Be the creator they find when they're looking to commit their attention.

Halloween and YouTube is a great example of this approach. Every year creators collaborate to try to own the internet by creating the best Halloween video. It's a challenge that has evolved and is now responsible for tens of millions of views for the platform at the end of October. And by understanding how the algorithm works, if you like watching one Halloween-themed video, then YouTube's recommended feature will serve a second and a third for you to enjoy whether or not you are subscribed to those channels. So this is a great way to get featured among bigger creators. Never be afraid to compete.

Watch how two of my favourite YouTubers, Jesse Wellens and Casey Neistat, take on Halloween.

Scan QR code to watch the videos

Trending/hashtags

Trending and hashtags are a great way to monitor what people are interested in. I am forever scanning Facebook, Google and Twitter advanced search to see what is not only attracting the attention of the world but also holding it. Reddit is another great place to keep an eye on — it's all insights and data. The beauty of social media is your ability to catch the waves as they take off. Often I will have a great idea for a video or I have even recorded and cut it and am just waiting for the trend to pop.

The rise of Pokémon Go is a classic example. While the game seized the attention of kids and teenagers worldwide, my aim was to attract the attention of marketers and corporate decision makers, the people who might hire me to speak or consult with them. As soon as the game started attracting viral view numbers and the streets were beginning to get crowded with phone zombies trying to catch Pikachu and the Snorlax, I went and recorded a video. But I didn't post it straight away. I held onto it. I waited until marketing managers and CEOs were being forced to take notice of this phenomenon and were then hungry to know more about a game they first suspected was going to be a passing distraction. The key is that I waited until my target audience were motivated by a desire before I posted the video publicly because that would result in them being more open to consuming it. I was feeding them when they were hungry for more.

I titled the video 'Pokémon Go explained'. I was solving the problem they were faced with, not knowing what this game was all about. The video was produced using the Virable formula with the aim of letting businesses understand how to monetise on the back of this emerging trend. I seeded it to my target market and off it went. Nearly 85 000 views from a starting base of 100 people.

Scan QR code
to watch the
video

There's nothing stopping you from executing the same strategy for the next cool thing that emerges. Now your voice is set, the approach and angles you need to take should be obvious even if it's just commentating and explaining a game that involves catching imaginary monsters. It certainly worked for a number of my real estate clients who are still remembered for the way they used Pokémon Go to draw attention to properties they had listed on the market.

Hashtags are a great way to get discovered. The beauty of them is that the right ones, the good ones, have already filtered out all the noise, and the people following them are primed for content that is well thought out and aligned. Work on your hashtags like you worked on your rules of engagement. The popular ones that are broad in topic and busy may look attractive statistically but it's a game of numbers. The more traffic, the more noise and the greater chance surrounding content on that hashtag is out of context, so the value of the hashtag in terms of gaining a return is reduced. Look to refine your selection to moderately busy tags where great content will stand out and get you noticed. You can also refine your audience by using a combination to deliver further context to your post. The perfect balance in terms of numbers varies, but if you are using more than five you need to sharpen your aim. And if you are continually using the same five you need to get more creative. Remember, the algorithms are always watching.

The key is to monitor trends and let them influence your creative ideas, but not to the point where you compromise your rules of engagement. By having a clear understanding of where you stand and what you stand for, you will be able to respond not only faster and more efficiently to trends but with a unique angle that is distinctly from your own Viral DNA. This will allow you to ride the wave of breaking trends and enjoy all the benefits that come from doing so without running out of control and damaging your reputation.

Music

Music is an interesting element in the video creation piece. If you are at the stage in your video-making journey where you are mastering your brand story, your rules are fairly robust, your storytelling techniques are returning positive reactions and you have a handle on the emotions and triggers you need to target, then the next step you can make to deliver the biggest impact is to incorporate music into your process.

Music can be a magical ingredient, but only once you have the foundations down and only if your chosen music ignites emotions that are aligned with the elements in the story you are sharing.

The power of music and the trigger effect it has on video comes in two forms: internal and external.

Internal

Internal triggers exist once the audience is already watching a video and how music is deployed influences emotional behaviour. But beware. As I briefly mention in chapter 10, music can either enhance or detract the level of emotional 'buy-in' an audience.

The brain is wired for allowing music to change its emotional state. Studies have shown music can reduce stress, pain and depression as well as improving cognitive and motor skills, and it even can produce its own neurons. Music has the ability to:

- **Influence life and in decision making by tapping into our emotional state.** Humans love consuming music just like they love consuming video so by successfully combining the two into one creative piece you will amplify and increase the rate in which the audience takes action.

- **Calm people down and trigger deeper feelings of sadness and loss, or hype an audience up and have them ready to run through brick walls.** It's important to choose what works best for the response you are aiming for.

- **Reduces the distraction of any unexpected background noises when run under videos of just you talking.** But I find it has the greatest impact for me when I use it, or the lack of it, to increase the impact of your overall lesson. I will often use music under the voiceovers of a lot of my 'speaking' videos (at a low volume to not detract from my dialogue) but then I cut it completely silent at the moment I deliver the video's key learnings. The silence triggers the viewer's brain to acknowledge a significant change in the environment and causes it to concentrate on what is happening, enhancing the impact of the lesson being shared.

For music to be a complimentary addition to a video it is important for the audio to match the video's pace. Translating that to the production and editing phase, once I have found a track that matches the mood of the video I am producing, I always let the music dictate my video edits. Fast-paced music needs to be matched with fast edits. The simple approach is to use the beat of the music as a guide for when to cut or change my shots. If the raw video you have recorded is made up of slow pans, tilts and time lapses, then it is going to be harder for me to match those shots to fast-paced music for a fast-paced edit, so you either have to find new music that aligns to the vision or you have to start again.

When I first started making videos finding the right paced music was a constant issue. Because I would always evolve and develop my idea as I went along, I ended up with a catalogue of uncomfortable to watch, disconnected videos. However, this doesn't happen to me anymore because my Rules of Engagement guide and keep me on track and on style with the type of video I am aiming to make, even if I am tempted to continually evolve and develop creative ideas.

External

The external triggers that come with music exist, in how if influences culture. In some cities around the world neighbourhood boundaries can be determined by the music coming from the houses on the block. Think of South Central Los Angeles compared with the neighbouring suburb of Hawthorne, near Manhattan beach. One is drenched in a history of hardcore Hip Hop music and culture, while the other is the birthplace of The Beach Boys and that Californian surfer laid-back feel.

This makes music a great way of identifying with and connecting to specific audience subsets based on both location and interests. Depending on what you have to sell and who you need to sell it to, the right music can be a significant external trigger to pique that initial interest.

Music also dictates trends. Right now, as I write this book, millions of tweens, teens and some adults are making videos on both TikTok and Instagram Reels based purely on which song or music style is trending today. Let that settle in. You can wake up and have no idea what you are going to do in your video that day, but after spending 10-15 minutes scanning the trending pages, and know the dance moves you need to execute and the song you need to perform to in order to attract the most views.

In that scenario, on those platforms, music is a complete external trigger.

In other ways, music influences trends around sport, fashion, art and culture in very much the same way that news and dates can. Music is like electricity weaved into the fabric of a society, so make sure you monitor it and leverage it in your videos when you can.

Integrate music successfully into your videos and the benefits will be obvious almost immediately.

*NOTE: Before you start going and using the latest billboard chart toppers as the soundtracks to you life's videos ensure you respect all copyright laws in the state in which you reside and those that exist on each individual social platform.

recap:
TIMING ISN'T EVERYTHING ...
BUT IT SURE IS SOMETHING

- Triggers increase relevancy and the rate in which you can influence a viewer's behaviour.

- Always be monitoring the mood, shifts and trends in your audience's environment and aligning your creative ideas to them.

- Your rules will guide you on which triggers to react to and how.

conclusion

Five years, 1200 viral videos, any number of late nights, four rewrites, one pursuit — to understand ...

Why do people share stuff?

That was the seed that started this incredible journey for me. At first I was chasing the answer to use when setting up a video production business. That changed as I started to work on my own brand story clarity, belief systems and mantras around the work I was conducting. My goal, I decided, was to save the internet ... one bad video at a time. Achieving that goal meant helping those who need it most and not just the people, businesses or brands with the most money.

This book, my keynotes and my courses are all geared to empowering the underdog to out-communicate, out-market and out-sell the bigger players.

The underdog narrative is my all-time favourite. In a lot of ways entrepreneurs, small and often even medium-sized businesses are underdogs, but that doesn't mean they have to play small. That's what makes the internet and social media such a magnificent opportunity for all of us right now. There are no barriers to entry. Everyone has an equal shot at success. And those set to win will be those who listened, connected and delivered better than the others.

Viral videos are the alpha predators of the internet, the most powerful force for capturing attention and driving mass consumption, yet often talk of them is laced with scepticism and mocking judgement. To the doubters I say this. If you are going to learn something new, you'd better learn from the best or you will simply be wasting time and money. Viral videos, I believe, are the greatest marketing phenomenon there has ever been.

It's just over 10 years since the first video broke the 1 million views barrier. That makes viral videos a relatively young phenomenon, and they are still widely misunderstood. For individuals and businesses that won't take the time to understand them and continue to place them in the too-hard basket, make no mistake, this is your opportunity.

If this book has helped to convey only a fraction of what videos can do for you or your business or to motivate you to make videos to begin with, you are already towards the front of the pack.

Social media isn't a fad, it's the new normal. The video era isn't coming, it's here.

And video is the format that delivers what social platforms crave. Action.

Actions = Data, and Data = Dollars

If you can help them make dollars it only makes sense that they will help you in return. It's business.

A forum on YouTube recently revealed that just 10 000 videos are responsible for more than 1 billion views on the platform, while more than 70 per cent of videos uploaded have fewer than 500 views. These figures clearly indicates a shortage of quality content because as a platform YouTube certainly isn't short of a user base.

Again, this is your opportunity, the chance to build an audience that in years to come will cost tens of thousands of dollars to procure, but right now they're sitting there waiting for you to find them for free.

I hope that, by better understanding the brain science that drives viral videos, the story structures that the brain craves and the triggers to get you noticed, this will give you the confidence you need to pick up a camera, to lift the performance of your videos not in spikes but comprehensively. There would be nothing more satisfying to me than to know that reading this book encouraged you to tell your own story. I promise that the investment you make in decoding your Viral DNA — the art and science of your most infectious story — will pay you back not only now but well into the future.

Social platforms are getting noisier but they are also getting smarter — smarter at recognising influential and powerful content, videos that tell stories over videos that sell stuff, videos that engage a community over videos that bore them stupid, videos that trigger actions over videos that cause people to put down their phones.

My aim is not only to open your mind to what's possible but to help show you a way that makes navigating the social media minefield a little easier. The fact you have stayed with me on this journey is your advantage. While most people are only just getting their heads around the question of whether video is a thing they should try, you've already unpacked the steps to producing videos with the Spread Factor — something that took me five years to identify and decode.

With the worlds of virtual and augmented reality video already upon us, you need to learn how to master 2D storytelling before you can even dream of telling stories in a 360-degree format. To paraphrase the great Walt Disney, now you have these tools and insights, never stand still, explore and experiment with the world of video, stay ahead of the pack and reap the benefits. You don't need expensive cameras — the one in your phone will do. You don't need expensive lighting — sunlight through the window is the best you can get. You don't need voice lessons — everyone's voice is unique.

I hope you embrace the opportunities that exist in the world of video. A place where everyone with a story to tell now has a platform from which to tell it. We are truly lucky.

As a kid I always dreamed of making movies, but I never had a camera. Now I carry an entire studio in my pocket, all I'm left with is excuses.

Find your voice, tell your story and share it with the world. And don't forget to Like, Comment, Share and BUY.

the Virable framework

I love surprises. I also love Easter eggs in video games — they are the little extras that are hidden away and only reveal themselves if you master or uncover a secret code. As you reach the end of this book, I want to honour this tradition.

You have no doubt been working on your brand story clarity, rules of engagement, storytelling techniques, emotional contagion and triggers, but you may be wondering how to apply them in a consistent, daily context to create great videos? To help the visual learners among you create awesome, kick-ass videos, I've developed a really simple framework that takes you through the thought process I use myself before committing to making a video. All you have to do is fill in the work you have already completed in this book, mount it somewhere everyone can see it, consume it daily and buy into it; remember, these are your values and beliefs. I know some people have even framed it.

Be sure to send me a video of yours going up and tag me on any social platform so I'm notified.

To access the Virable framework simply scan this code and download it.

Scan QR code to access the framework

It's been awesome sharing your attention and I look forward to you holding mine.

Peace.

P.S. If you had any trouble with the QR codes in this book, visit **www.likecommentsharebuy.com/bonuses** to access the videos and frameworks directly.

about the author

Jonathan Creek is an award-winning investigative journalist, international speaker, TED speaker and internet filmmaker. He works with individuals, entrepreneurs and start-up businesses as well as corporate teams and multinationals in the areas of brand story, video and social strategy.

Jonathan is a recognised authority in the video strategy, social communications and viral content space, helping his clients to simplify complex messages into easily consumable stories of influence that attract attention and trigger the right actions to drive instant, long-lasting business results.

Jonathan lives with his wife, Brittany, and their two children in Melbourne's leafy eastern suburbs.

If you are looking for an energised, powerful keynote presenter, conference emcee/host, workshop facilitator or coach, connect with Jonathan at virable.com.

index